CLERKENWELL & ISLINGTON PUBS

JOHNNY HOMER

AMBERLEY

This book is dedicated to my good friends Stevie Cox and Alan Higham, who over many years accompanied me during my research into the public houses of Clerkenwell and Islington. It was fun while it lasted.

First published 2017

Amberley Publishing
The Hill, Stroud
Gloucestershire, GL5 4EP

www.amberley-books.com

ISBN 978 1 4456 6330 2 (print)
ISBN 978 1 4456 6331 9 (ebook)

British Library Cataloguing in Publication Data.
A catalogue record for this book is available from the British Library.

Origination by Amberley Publishing.
Printed in the UK.

Contents

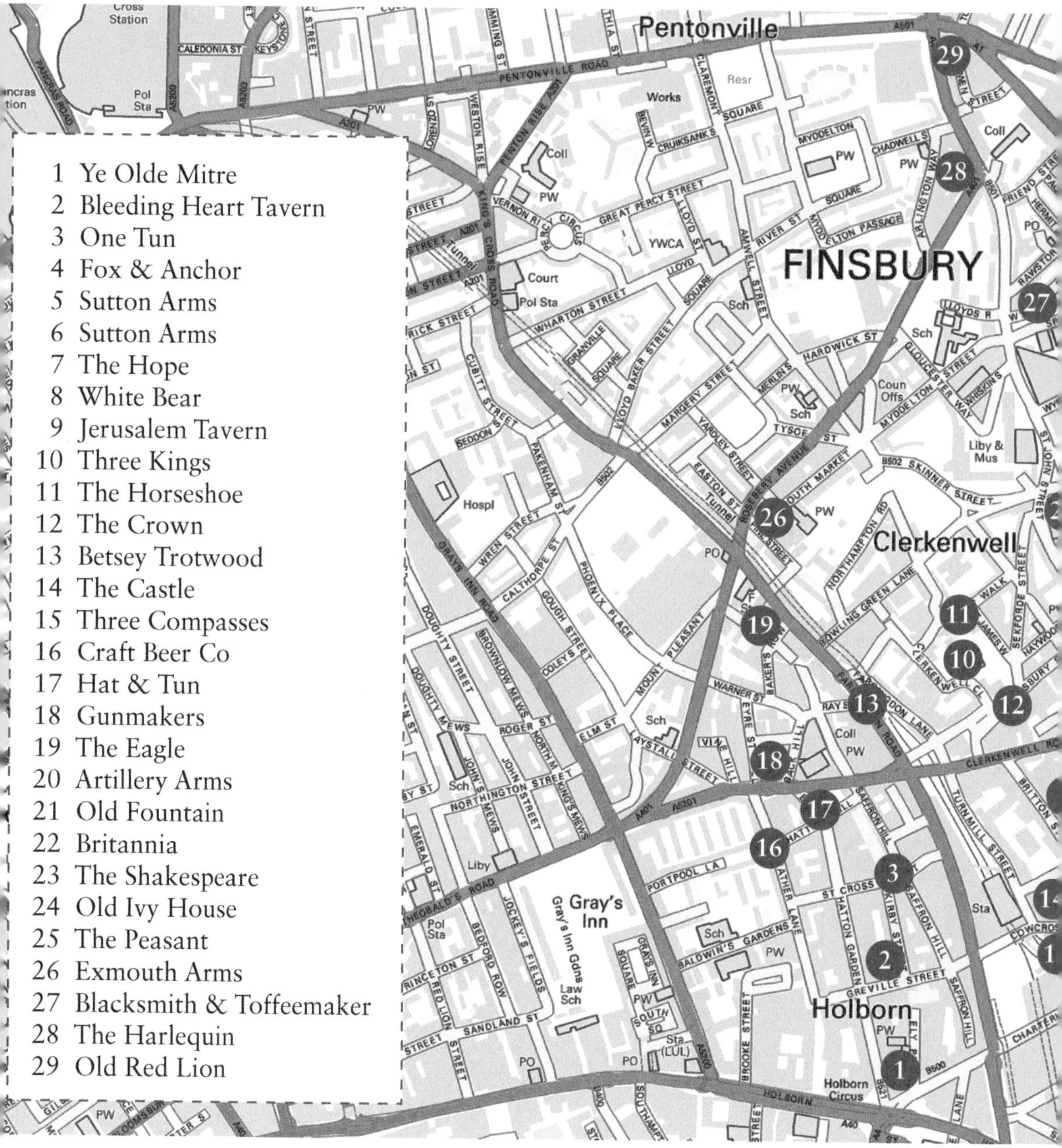

1 Ye Olde Mitre
2 Bleeding Heart Tavern
3 One Tun
4 Fox & Anchor
5 Sutton Arms
6 Sutton Arms
7 The Hope
8 White Bear
9 Jerusalem Tavern
10 Three Kings
11 The Horseshoe
12 The Crown
13 Betsey Trotwood
14 The Castle
15 Three Compasses
16 Craft Beer Co
17 Hat & Tun
18 Gunmakers
19 The Eagle
20 Artillery Arms
21 Old Fountain
22 Britannia
23 The Shakespeare
24 Old Ivy House
25 The Peasant
26 Exmouth Arms
27 Blacksmith & Toffeemaker
28 The Harlequin
29 Old Red Lion

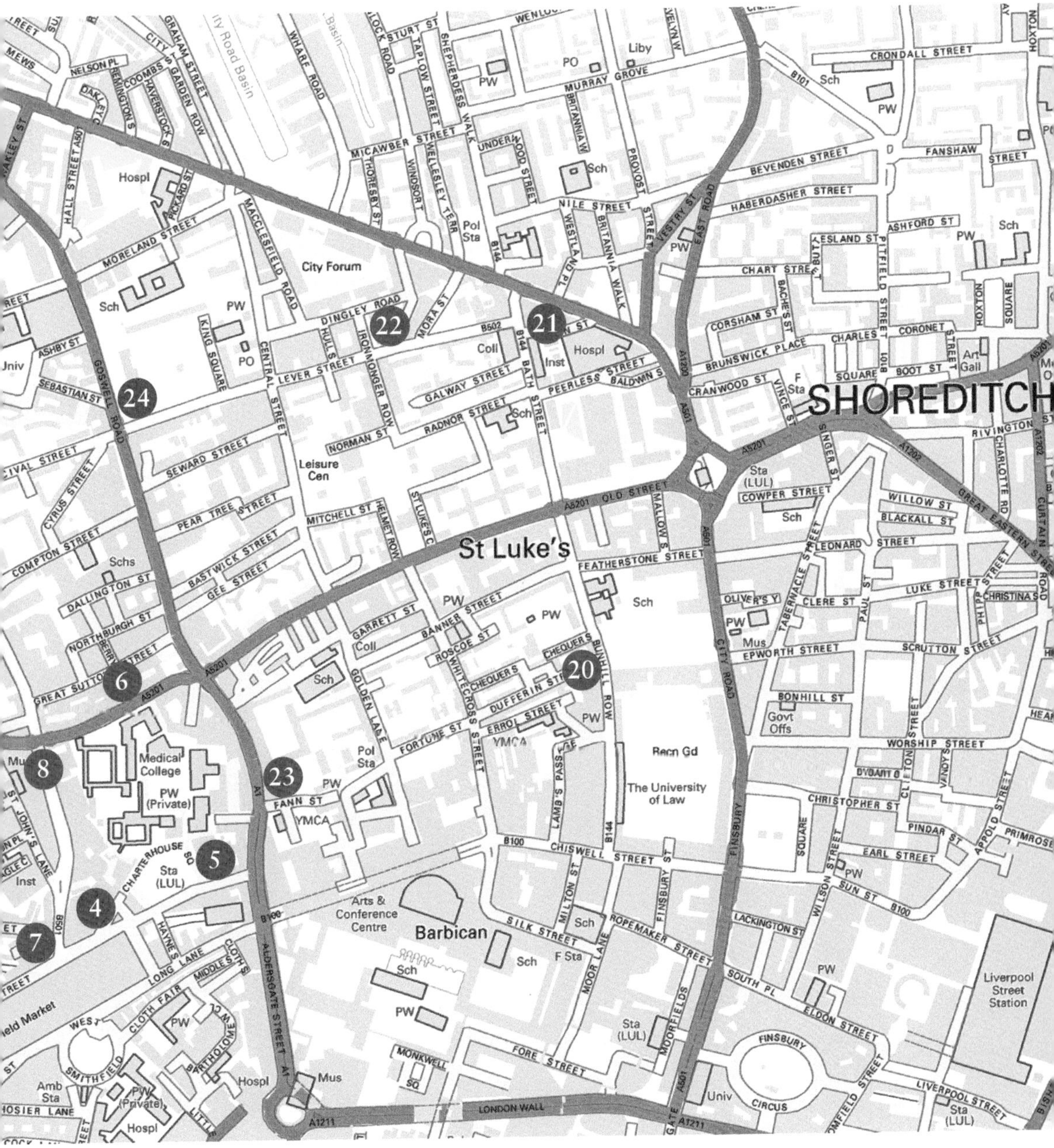

SHOREDITCH
St Luke's
Barbican
City Forum
Leisure Cen
Arts & Conference Centre
Medical College
The University of Law
Recn Gd
Liverpool Street Station
Smithfield
City Road Basin
GOSWELL ROAD
CITY ROAD
OLD STREET
EAST ROAD
ALDERSGATE STREET
LONDON WALL
FINSBURY
FINSBURY CIRCUS
GREAT EASTERN STREET
CHISWELL STREET
SILK STREET
ROPEMAKER STREET
MOOR LANE
MOORFIELDS
FORE STREET
MONKWELL SQ
GOLDEN LANE
WHITECROSS STREET
BUNHILL ROW
CHEQUERS
DUFFERIN ST
ERROL STREET
FORTUNE ST
FANN ST
BANNER STREET
ROSCOE ST
GARRETT ST
LAMB'S PASS
MILTON ST
FEATHERSTONE STREET
MALLOW S
BATH STREET
RADNOR STREET
GALWAY STREET
NORMAN ST
MITCHELL ST
HELMET ROW
IRONMONGER ROW
LEVER STREET
DINGLEY ROAD
HULLS
MORA ST
CENTRAL STREET
KING SQUARE
MACCLESFIELD ROAD
MORELAND STREET
WHARF ROAD
GRAHAM STREET
CITY GARDEN ROW
HAVERSTOCK S
COOMBS S
REMINGTON S
NELSON PL
PICKARD ST
HALL STREET
ASHBY ST
SEBASTIAN ST
SEWARD STREET
PEAR TREE STREET
BASTWICK STREET
GEE STREET
DALLINGTON ST
NORTHBURGH ST
COMPTON STREET
CYRUS STREET
GREAT SUTTON STREET
CHARTERHOUSE SQ
LONG LANE
HAYNE S
CLOTH FAIR
MIDDLE S
WEST SMITHFIELD
HOSIER LANE
ST JOHN'S LANE
MICAWBER STREET
WINDSOR
THORESBY ST
WELLESLEY TERR
TAPLOW STREET
SHEPHERDESS WALK
STURT ST
MURRAY GROVE
UNDERWOOD STREET
NILE STREET
BRITANNIA WALK
WESTLAND PL
PROVOST STREET
VESTRY ST
BEVENDEN STREET
HABERDASHER STREET
CHART STREET
CORSHAM ST
BRUNSWICK PLACE
PEERLESS STREET
BALDWIN S
CRANWOOD ST
VINCE ST
BACHES ST
PITFIELD STREET
CHARLES SQUARE
CORONET STREET
BOOT ST
ASHFORD ST
FANSHAW STREET
CRONDALL STREET
HOXTON SQUARE
RIVINGTON ST
CHARLOTTE RD
CURTAIN ROAD
COWPER STREET
WILLOW ST
BLACKALL ST
LEONARD STREET
TABERNACLE STREET
PAUL ST
CLERE ST
LUKE STREET
CHRISTINA S
OLIVER'S Y
EPWORTH STREET
SCRUTTON STREET
BONHILL ST
WORSHIP STREET
CHRISTOPHER ST
CLIFTON STREET
PINDAR ST
EARL STREET
APPOLD STREET
PRIMROSE
SUN ST
WILSON STREET
LACKINGTON ST
SOUTH PL
ELDON STREET
LIVERPOOL STREET
SQUARE
Sch
PW
PO
Liby
Hospl
Pol Sta
Coll
Inst
F Sta
Sta (LUL)
YMCA
Mus
Govt Offs
Art Gall
Univ
Amb Sta
PW (Private)
A501
A5201
A1
A1211
A1200
A1202
B100
B144
B502
B101
24
22
21
20
23
6
8
5
4
7

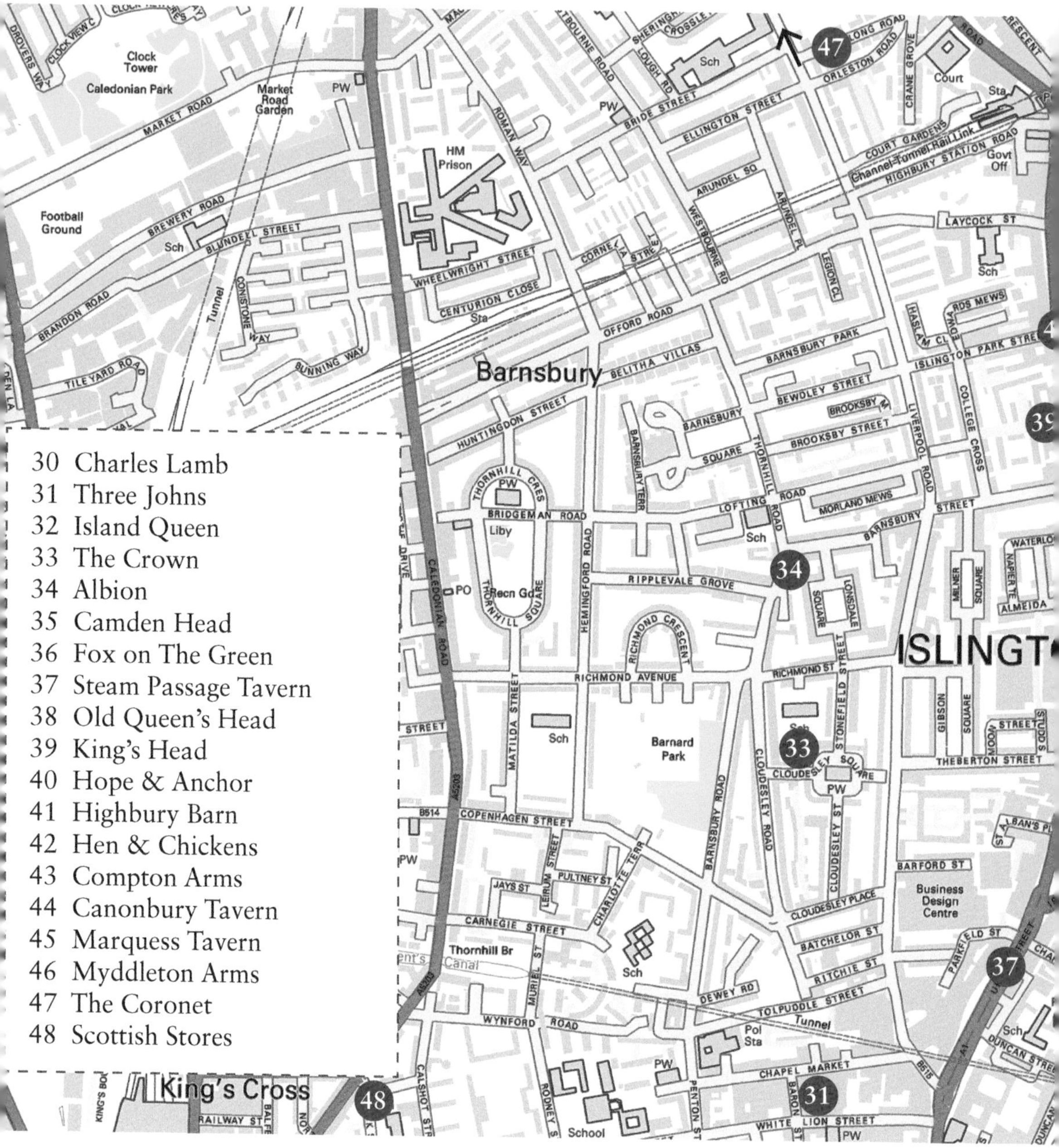
30 Charles Lamb
31 Three Johns
32 Island Queen
33 The Crown
34 Albion
35 Camden Head
36 Fox on The Green
37 Steam Passage Tavern
38 Old Queen's Head
39 King's Head
40 Hope & Anchor
41 Highbury Barn
42 Hen & Chickens
43 Compton Arms
44 Canonbury Tavern
45 Marquess Tavern
46 Myddleton Arms
47 The Coronet
48 Scottish Stores
Barnsbury
ISLINGT
King's Cross
Clock Tower
Caledonian Park
Market Road Garden
HM Prison
Football Ground
Barnard Park
Business Design Centre
Thornhill Br
Court
Channel Tunnel Rail Link
Market Road
Brewery Road
Blundell Street
Brandon Road
Tileyard Road
Caledonian Road
Roman Way
Wheelwright Street
Centurion Close
Offord Road
Belitha Villas
Huntingdon Street
Thornhill Crescent
Thornhill Square
Bridgeman Road
Hemingford Road
Ripplevale Grove
Richmond Crescent
Richmond Avenue
Matilda Street
Copenhagen Street
Carnegie Street
Wynford Road
Barnsbury Road
Cloudesley Road
Cloudesley Square
Stonefield Street
Lonsdale Square
Thornhill Road
Barnsbury Square
Barnsbury Park
Bewdley Street
Brooksby Street
Liverpool Road
College Cross
Islington Park Street
Theberton Street
Barford St
Chapel Market
White Lion Street
Tolpuddle Street
Penton St
Caledonian Road
Bride Street
Ellington Street
Orleston Road
Long Road
Highbury Station Road
Laycock St
Arundel Sq
Westbourne Rd
Calshot St
Railway St

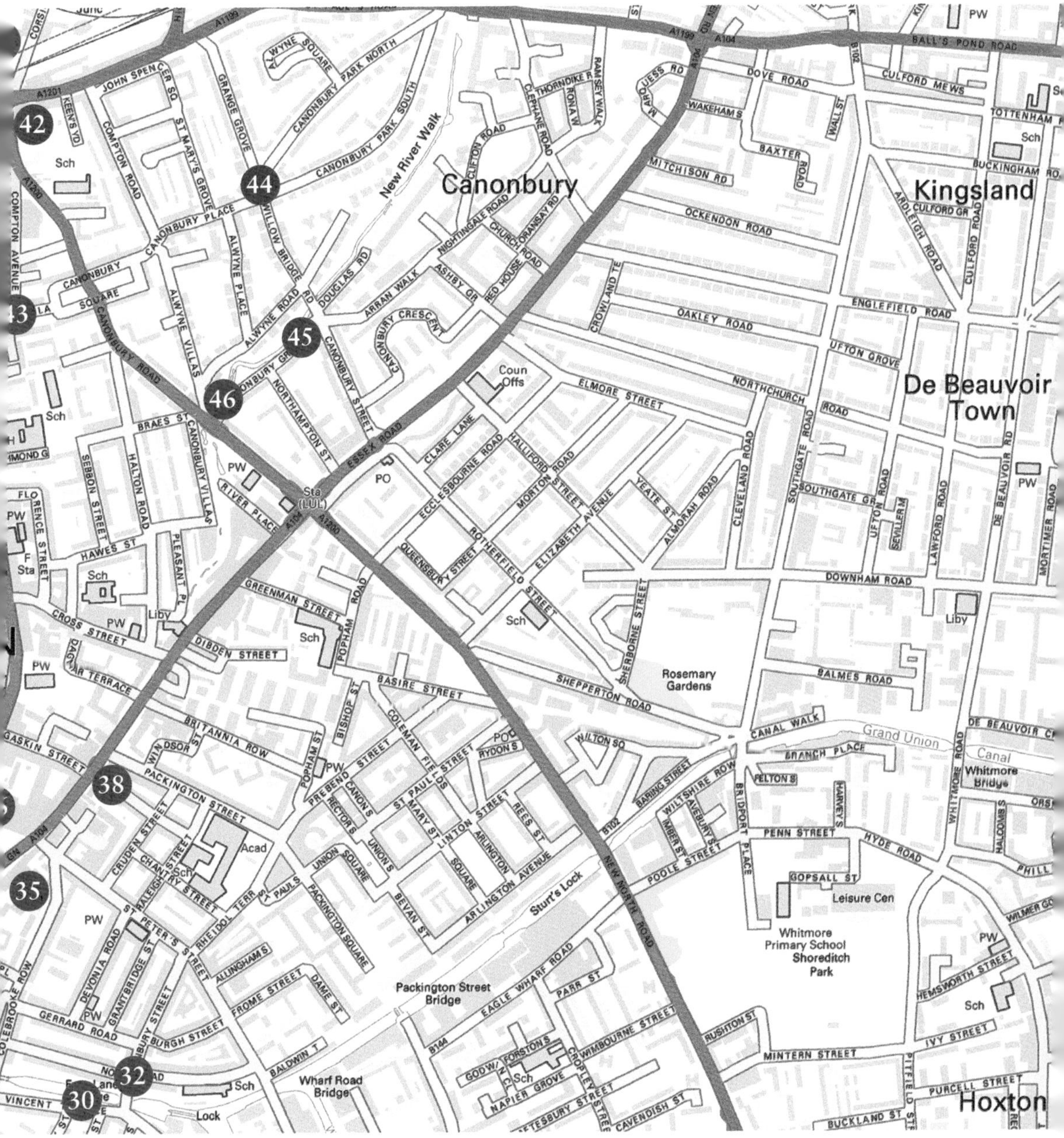

Canonbury
Kingsland
De Beauvoir Town
Hoxton
42
43
44
45
46
38
35
32
30
BALL'S POND ROAD
DOVE ROAD
CULFORD MEWS
TOTTENHAM
BUCKINGHAM
WAKEHAM S
BAXTER ROAD
MITCHISON RD
OCKENDON ROAD
CULFORD GR
ARDLEIGH ROAD
CULFORD ROAD
ENGLEFIELD ROAD
OAKLEY ROAD
CROWLAND TE
UFTON GROVE
NORTHCHURCH ROAD
ELMORE STREET
Coun Offs
CLARE LANE
ECCLESBOURNE ROAD
HALLIFORD STREET
MORTON ROAD
ELIZABETH AVENUE
YEATE ST
ALMORAH ROAD
CLEVELAND ROAD
SOUTHGATE ROAD
SOUTHGATE GR
UFTON ROAD
SEVILLE M
LAWFORD ROAD
DE BEAUVOIR RD
MORTIMER ROAD
DOWNHAM ROAD
Liby
BALMES ROAD
Rosemary Gardens
SHERBORNE STREET
SHEPPERTON ROAD
CANAL WALK
Grand Union Canal
BRANCH PLACE
DE BEAUVOIR C
Whitmore Bridge
WHITMORE ROAD
HALCOMB S
FELTON S
WILTSHIRE ROW
BARING STREET
WILTON SQ
BRIDPORT PLACE
HARVEY S
PENN STREET
HYDE ROAD
GOPSALL ST
Leisure Cen
Whitmore Primary School
Shoreditch Park
WILMER GD
HEMSWORTH STREET
IVY STREET
MINTERN STREET
RUSHTON ST
PITFIELD ST
PURCELL STREET
BUCKLAND ST
NEW NORTH ROAD
POOLE STREET
Sturt's Lock
JOHN SPENCER SQ
KEEN'S YD
COMPTON ROAD
COMPTON AVENUE
ST MARY'S GROVE
GRANGE GROVE
ALWYNE SQUARE
CANONBURY PARK NORTH
CANONBURY PARK SOUTH
New River Walk
CLIFTON ROAD
THORNDIKE R
CLEPHANE ROAD
RAMSEY WALK
RONA W
MARQUESS RD
CANONBURY PLACE
ALWYNE PLACE
WILLOW BRIDGE RD
NIGHTINGALE ROAD
CHURCH ROAD
ORANSAY RD
DOUGLAS RD
ASHBY GR
RED HOUSE
ARRAN WALK
CANONBURY CRESCENT
CANONBURY SQUARE
ALWYNE ROAD
ALWYNE VILLAS
CANONBURY ROAD
CANONBURY STREET
NORTHAMPTON ST
CANONBURY VILLAS
ESSEX ROAD
BRAES ST
SEBBON STREET
HALTON ROAD
FLORENCE STREET
RIVER PLACE
Sta (LUL)
PO
HAWES ST
PLEASANT PL
GREENMAN STREET
POPHAM ROAD
QUEENSBURY STREET
ROTHERFIELD STREET
CROSS STREET
DIBDEN STREET
DAGMAR TERRACE
BASIRE STREET
BISHOP ST
COLEMAN FIELDS
BRITANNIA ROW
WINDSOR ST
GASKIN STREET
POPHAM ST
PREBEND STREET
RYDON S
ST PAUL'S ST
CANON S
RECTOR S
ST MARY ST
LINTON STREET
REES ST
ARLINGTON SQUARE
ARLINGTON AVENUE
UNION SQUARE
PACKINGTON STREET
CRUDEN STREET
CHANTRY STREET
RALEIGH STREET
Acad
RHEIDOL TERR
PACKINGTON SQUARE
BEVAN ST
ST PETER'S STREET
DEVONIA ROAD
GRANTBRIDGE ST
ALLINGHAM S
FROME STREET
DAME ST
COLEBROOKE ROW
GERRARD ROAD
BURGH STREET
Packington Street Bridge
EAGLE WHARF ROAD
PARR ST
WIMBOURNE STREET
BALDWIN T
Wharf Road Bridge
FORSTON S
GODWIN C
NAPIER GROVE
SHAFTESBURY STREET
CROPLEY STREET
CAVENDISH ST
VINCENT
Lock
Sch
PW

Introduction

I have spent the majority of my life living in Clerkenwell and Islington, growing up with an EC1 postcode. These are two of London's most engaging, diverse and metropolitan districts, rich in history and hotbeds of radicalism. This history, and to an extent this radicalism, is reflected in many of the area's pubs.

I have probably been 'researching' this book since I was first old enough to cross the threshold and enter the wonderful, and occasionally weird, world of the English public house. Alas, as an institution the pub has taken a bit of a battering in recent years, and many of the watering holes I remember from my younger days have sadly now gone or been changed almost beyond recognition.

I was always rather fond, for instance, of the old Crown and Woolpack in St John Street, a handsome pub that always looked rather battered around the edges. It was here in 1905 that Lenin met with fellow exiled members of the Russian Social Democratic Labour Party, an occasion when a plain clothes policeman from the Met hid in a cupboard to eavesdrop on proceedings, all of which took place in Russian, much to the bafflement of the officer concerned. The last time I looked the Crown and Woolpack was a hair salon.

I also remember well the first time I walked into a pub as a paying customer. I undertook this most momentous chapter in my life alongside my dad, and it was at his invitation that I did so. He bought me a pint on that fateful day, and then I bought him one back. The pub in question was the George and Dragon in St John Street, a Truman's house if my memory serves me right and a grand old Victorian boozer that now proclaims itself the Peasant.

Clerkenwell

Clerkenwell is perhaps the place I love most on this earth. It is a truly unique place with a truly unique atmosphere and as one walks its ancient lanes and alleyways, the sense of history is sometimes almost tangible. The area takes its name from an ancient water source, the Clerks' Well, which is recorded here as early as the twelfth century.

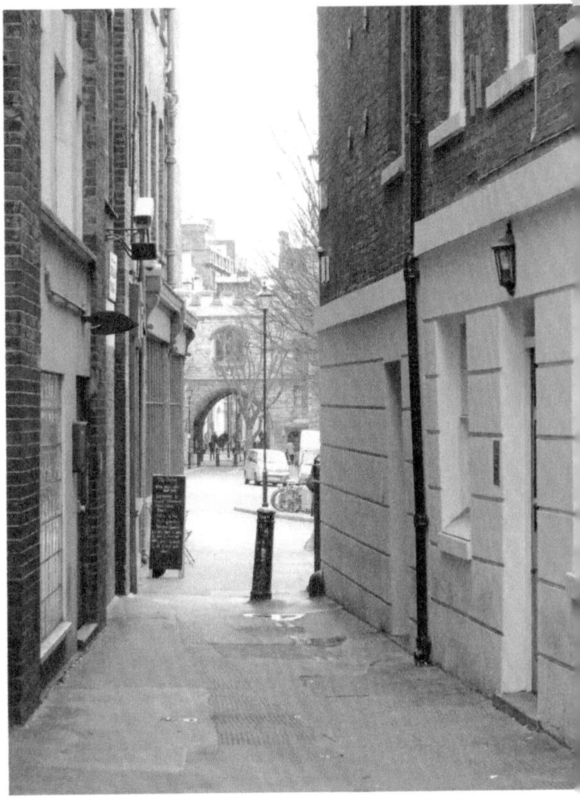

The sense of history in Clerkenwell's many alleyways and lanes is almost tangible.

During the Middle Ages it was the location for the annual mystery plays performed by members of the Worshipful Company of Parish Clerks. The well was 'rediscovered' in 1924 in the basement of offices in Farringdon Lane then occupied by the *New Statesman* magazine. Today it can still be seen, now located beneath a 1980s office block calling itself, rather aptly, Well Court.

Clerkenwell was also the home of the Knights Hospitallers of St John of Jerusalem and the sixteenth-century St John's Gate can still be seen today, as can the remains of St John's Church in St John's Square. Today the gate houses the museum of the Order of St John.

Over the years Clerkenwell has, as mentioned earlier, been a hotbed of radicalism and the Marx Memorial Library can be found in Clerkenwell Green. Across the busy Farringdon Road, meanwhile, for almost a hundred years from 1850 onwards was London's Little Italy. London's Italian population started to leave the area in the 1960s, but the annual Procession of Our Lady of Mount Carmel still takes place here every July, centred on St Peter's Italian Church.

Islington

Today's London Borough of Islington is a sprawling affair, sharing a border with Haringey to the north, the City to the south, Hackney to the east and Camden to the west. In terms of area it is the second smallest of the capital's boroughs, after Kensington and Chelsea, but what it lacks in size it more than makes up for in history and character. Once a mostly rural area outside the City proper, Islington was a place where Londoners came to take fresh 'country' air and visit grand pleasure gardens.

As the main route from the north into the City, the amount of traffic passing through Islington saw a rapid growth in the number of taverns and inns, among them the famous Angel Inn, later Angel Hotel, on the corner of Islington High Street and Pentonville Road, which would also give its name to the immediate neighbourhood we know today.

After much development of squares and terraces started in the late eighteenth century, the population of Islington started to grow. For much of the twentieth century, however, it was a largely rundown area until gentrification, starting in the 1960s, slowly transformed it into the fashionable and cosmopolitan district of today. Over the years many pubs have disappeared, but many remain.

Finally, a quick note on the areas covered by this book. Clerkenwell, which as a district is quite amorphous these days, was a parish in its own right until 1900 when, alongside neighbouring St Luke's, it formed the old Metropolitan Borough of Finsbury. Finsbury, alas, was absorbed by the London Borough of Islington in 1965. What that means is that most of today's Clerkenwell now comes under the control of Islington, although some fringe parts to the north, south and west are actually in the London Borough of Camden.

The Angel Hotel, built in 1903 on the site of the old Angel Inn, now houses offices and a bank.

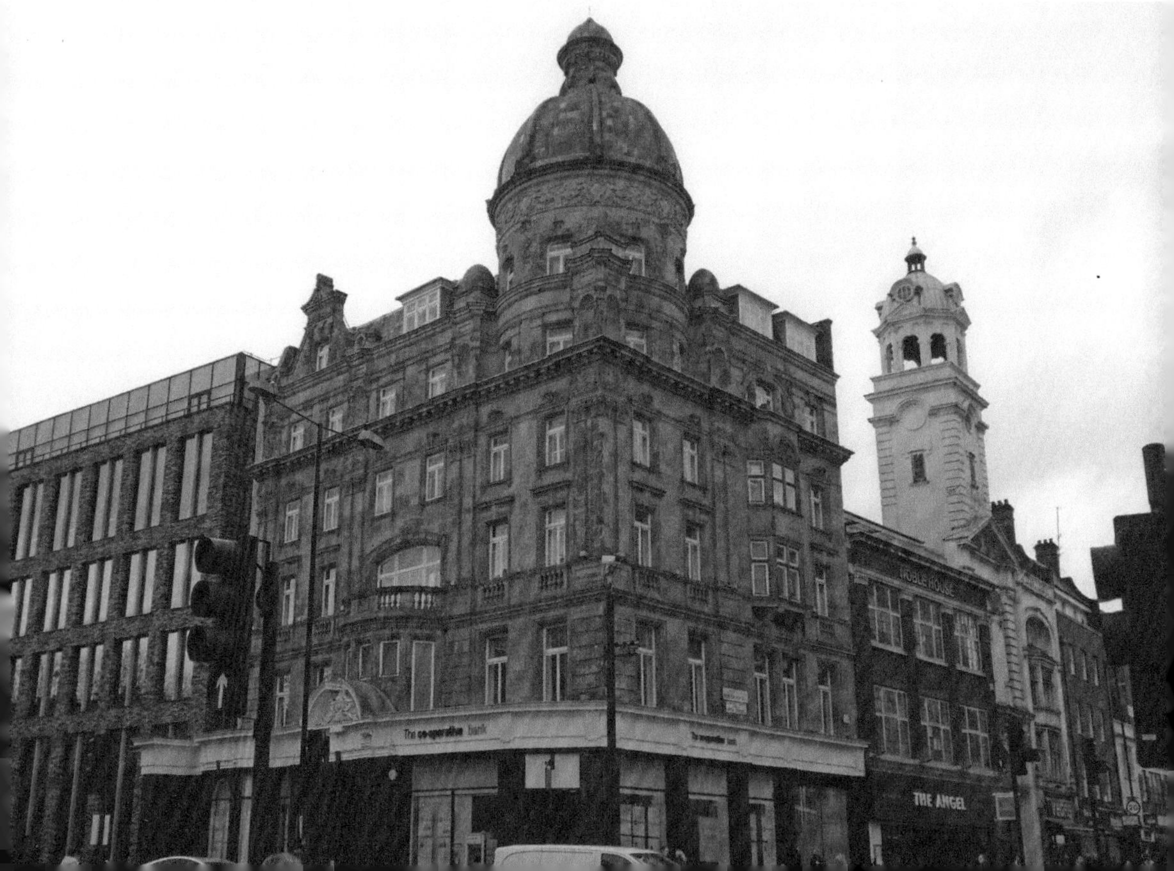

I

Clerkenwell

1. YE OLDE MITRE, No. 1 Ely Court, EC1

If you're looking to get away from the hustle and bustle of central London for an hour (or two?) then head for Hatton Garden where, if you are lucky, you'll find a crooked lamp post pointing to a narrow alleyway. This will lead in turn to Ely Court, and here you will find Ye Olde Mitre Tavern, truly one of London's most historic hostelries.

The earliest date we have for a tavern on this site is 1546, although the bare bones of the current pub date from 1772. There has, clearly, been many changes to the building

A crooked lamp post points the way to Ely Court and Ye Olde Mitre.

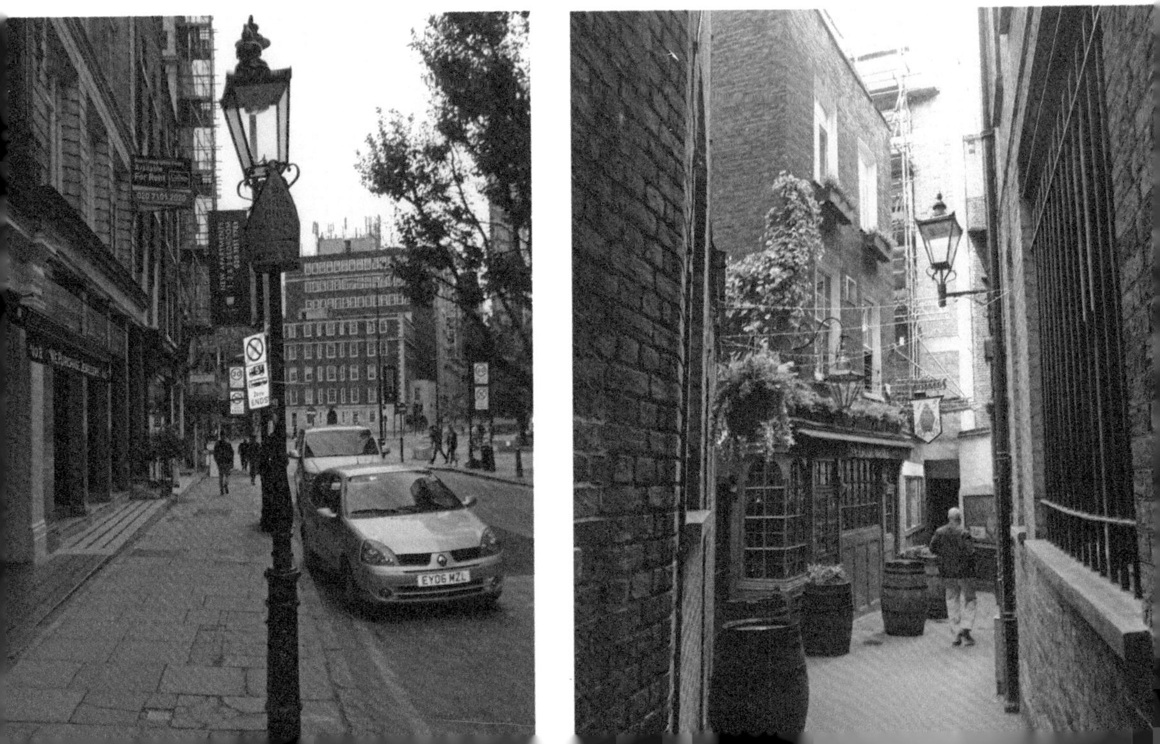

since but the most dramatic are internal, notably a refitting in the 1930s when some lovely wooden panelling was installed. The pub has enjoyed listed status since 1951.

This tiny part of London was once the London seat of the Bishop of Ely. His grand palace and chapel stood here from the thirteenth century on and it even gets a mention in Shakespeare's *Richard III*. For many years the area was, de facto, a tiny part of Cambridgeshire in the very heart of London and the Metropolitan Police could only enter Ely Place and its environs if invited to – although that is no longer the case.

Cherry Tree

The Mitre itself was most likely built as a place where servants working in the palace could take refuge and quaff a tankard or two of ale. These days, in addition to the upstairs Bishop's Room, the ground floor is divided into two separate bars, with a larger area to the rear and a smaller, more intimate one to the front. In the corner of this bar, encased in glass, is an aged piece of wood that is believed to be part of a cherry tree that originally stood here. An adjacent sign reads: 'Built by Bishop Goodrich in 1546. The Cherry Tree marks the boundary between the bishop's garden and the part leased to Sir Christopher Hatton.'

The more romantically inclined claim that this was the same cherry tree around which a young Elizabeth I danced while romantically linked with Hatton. She was in love; who

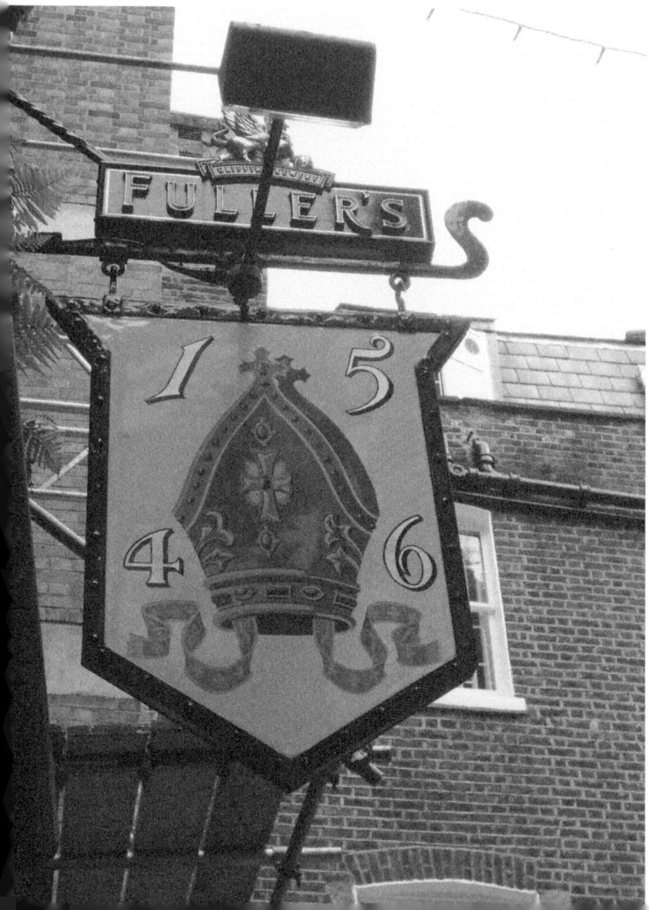

Ye Olde Mitre was first established in 1546.

can blame her for wanting to dance? It was the Virgin Queen who had insisted that Hatton be granted land here and if Goodrich did 'lease' it to Hatton, he did so very reluctantly.

The Mitre, now in the hands of Fuller's, remains one of the capital's great unspoilt pubs. It can get very busy at times, but choose your moment carefully and a visit here will not disappoint.

2. THE ONE TUN, No. 125 Saffron Hill, EC1

There are many London pubs in which Charles Dickens is supposed to have stopped off and supped during his intrepid perambulations around the Great Wen, but only a few of them can claim to have been immortalised in prose by the great man.

Such a pub is The One Tun, a solid and imposing old boozer in Saffron Hill, historic thoroughfare that takes its name from the crocuses (saffron is obtained from the calyx of the yellow crocus flower) once cultivated nearby on an industrial scale and used to disguise rancid meat. Saffron Hill these days seems a perpetually gloomy thoroughfare only rarely troubled by sunlight, and I suggest you'd struggled to grow so much as a tomato here now.

Certainly when Dickens knew the area, and he got to know it well, it was one of London's most notorious rookeries. It is here where Fagin had his lair in *Oliver Twist*. The fact that Dickens was prepared to explore the neighbourhood on foot is testament to both his inquisitive nature and sheer sense of fearlessness, especially when one considers 1850's *Hand-Book of London*, in which Peter Cunningham points out that local clergymen 'have been obliged, when visiting it [Saffron Hill], to be accompanied by policemen in plain clothes'.

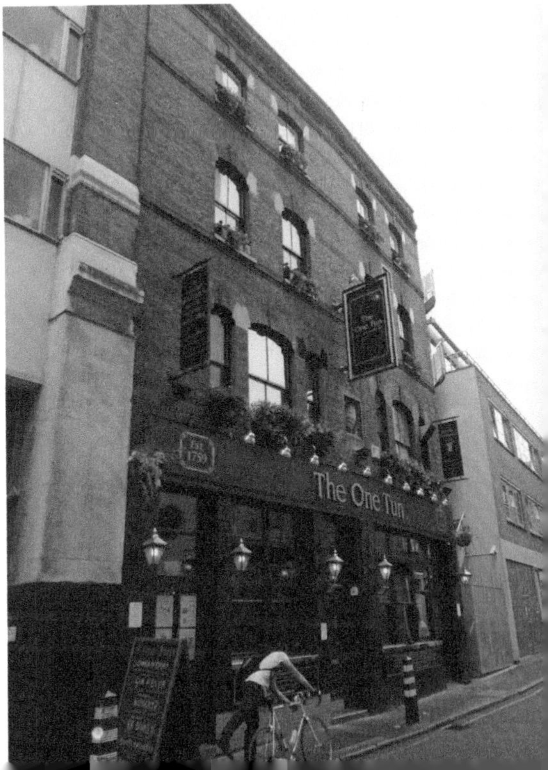

Charles Dickens immortalised The One Tun as the Three Cripples in *Oliver Twist*.

Oliver Twist

It is widely believed that The One Tun appears in *Oliver Twist* as the Three Cripples, a veritable den of vice and iniquity in which Fagin, based on the real-life Jewish 'fence' Ikey Solomons, and Bill Sykes – 'A man in a velveteen coat' – would drink and scheme and do business. However, it is widely accepted that the Three Cripples was actually a 'lodging house' without a licence to sell liquor, located directly next door to The One Tun. But then who would begrudge Dickens a little artistic licence in the blurring of fact and fiction?

Records show The One Tun has stood as an alehouse on this site since 1759. *Oliver Twist* was first published in serial form between 1837 and 1839 and Dickens would have known the pub from earlier the same decade, when larger-than-life landlord William Dixie ruled the roost. It would have been a rough and ready place at the time.

The current building dates from 1875 and to this day bears the enigmatic initials 'A. E' – the builder one assumes. It is one of only two pubs in London to bear The One Tun name – the other is located in Goodge Street, Fitzrovia. A tun was the largest measurement of barrel used for the storage, and occasionally transportation, of both beer and wine. A tun held 225 gallons, which is 1,800 pints of ale. Victorian London was clearly a very thirsty place.

3. BLEEDING HEART TAVERN, No. 1 Bleeding Heart Yard, EC1

Hatton Garden, on the fringes of what with a little geographical licence we can today declare Clerkenwell, has for many years been the centre of the UK diamond trade, so given the prevalence of precious jewels in the area, it comes as no surprise that today's Bleeding Heart Tavern is an unashamedly upmarket boozer. However its name,

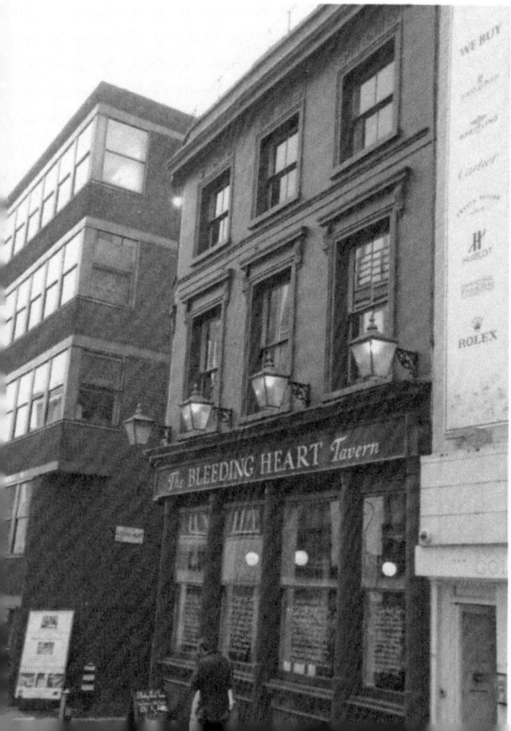

Bleeding Heart Tavern, Bleeding Heart Yard.

and that of Bleeding Heart Yard just around the corner, have their origins in one of London's very darkest legends.

There has been a tavern by the name of the Bleeding Heart here since at least 1746, when a Roger Hebden was listed as licensee. He was, the records tell us, 'a gentleman with no criminal convictions'. Good thing too, for this area was one of London's most notorious rookeries and a calm, cool head would have been needed at times to keep order.

It is almost certain that Dickens was familiar with the pub, for he knew the area very well. The One Tun, just around the corner in Saffron Hill, was the inspiration for the Three Cripples in *Oliver Twist* while Bleeding Heart Yard is where the Plornish family live in *Little Dorritt*. The square was, wrote Dickens, 'inhabited by poor people, who set up their rest among its faded glories as Arabs of the desert pitch their tents among the fallen stones of the Pyramids'.

Bloody Legend

The legend of Bleeding Heart Yard is rather a grisly one, as sometimes only London legend can be. It centres on Lady Elizabeth Hatton, widowed wife of Sir William Newport, nephew of Sir Christopher Hatton. Newport adopted the Hatton name upon his uncle's death. Lady Hatton was a well-known figure in seventeenth-century London high society and, it was rumoured, had entered into a pact with the Devil so as to advance her late husband's career.

On January 26 1626, she organised a grand Winter Ball and guests were enraptured when she took to the floor with a mysterious figure, a 'swarthy gentleman' who many took to be the Spanish Ambassador, with whom she had previously enjoyed a romantic engagement. The two soon walked outside, for a breath of fresh air no doubt.

The following morning, so legend goes, Lady Hatton's body was found in the nearby yard, mutilated and very dead but with her heart still somehow pumping blood onto the glistening cobblestones. Was it the Spanish Ambassador with whom she had left the ball? Or was it the Devil, who had come for payment?

The reality is rather different. She actually died of natural causes, aged sixty-eight. Not a bad innings at all for the time.

4. FOX & ANCHOR, No. 115 Charterhouse Street, EC1

The Fox & Anchor is more than just a pub; it's an art nouveau gem that attracts admirers from near and far. It once catered for market porters from nearby Smithfield Meat Market, but these days attracts a mix of suited City types and some of the area's growing population of media and design hepcats. London is a city in a constant state of flux, and this area is, for better or worse, changing more than most.

The pub has the distinct air of a City hostelry about it, from its 7 a.m. weekday opening time through to the rush hour crush of the ground-floor bar, but technically this elegant and slightly aloof dame of a boozer is actually located on the eastern fringes of Clerkenwell, technically sitting in the London Borough of Islington.

A pub has stood on this site for at least 200 years, and there are records of the Fox & Anchor here as early as the 1780s. The current building was built between 1897

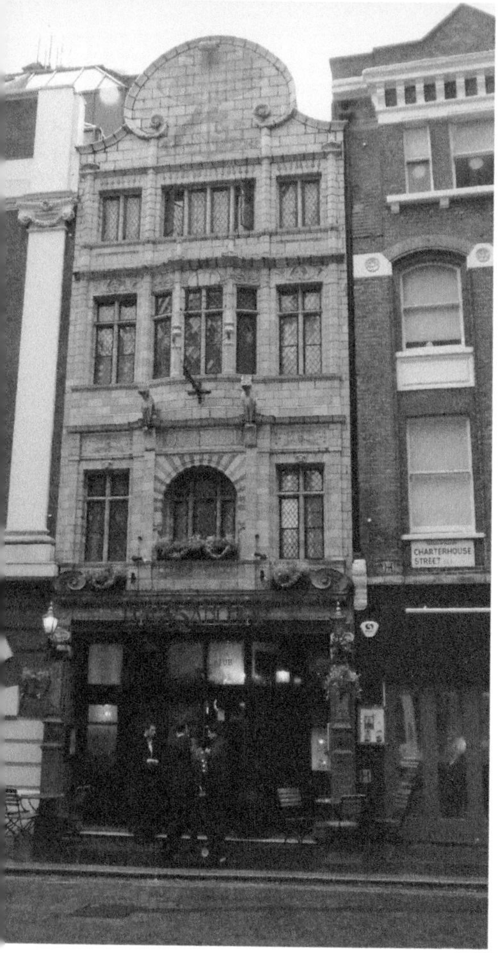

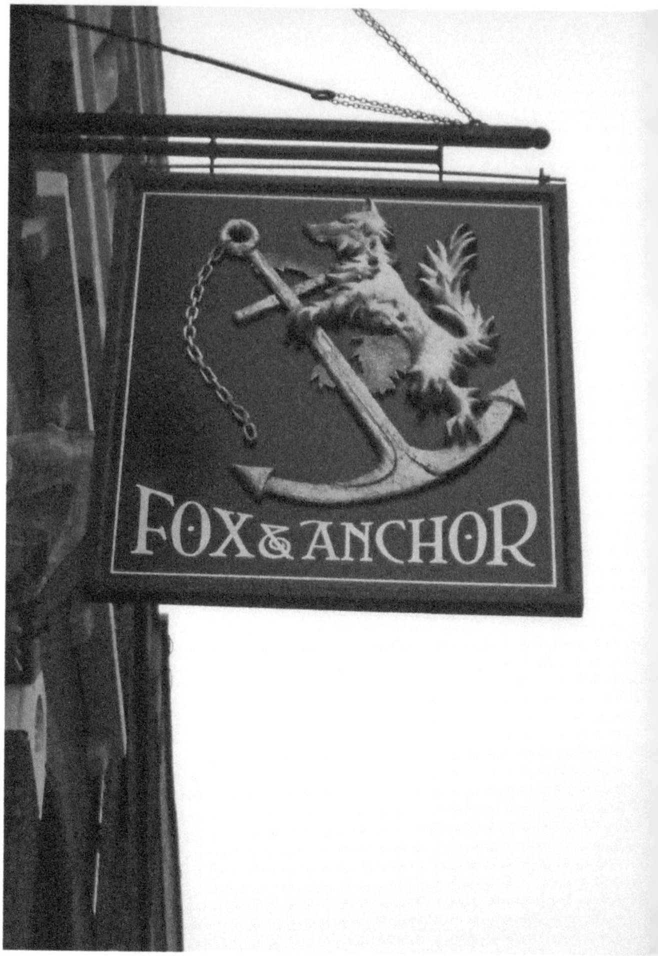

The Fox & Anchor, Smithfield, is an art nouveau gem.

and 1899, designed by Lambeth-born architect Latham Augustus Withall. Outside it features some sumptuous cut glass and a pair of gargoyles. The real star of the show, however, are the ornate tiles, the work of William J. Neatby. Perhaps Neatby's best-known legacy was the interior of Harrods' food hall.

Early Licence

The pub has been Grade II listed since 1972 and in 1993 was awarded a CAMRA/English Heritage Pub Conservation Award, but in 2006 it closed its doors and remained closed into the following year. For a while the ground-floor entrance was boarded up – a worrying sign for both pub aficionados and lovers of good design alike.

However there is a very happy end to this story, for the pub now thrives in the hands of Young's, formerly of Wandsworth. They carried out a sympathetic refurbishment of the Fox and, as a result, it now leads something of a double, if not treble, life as a pub, gastropub and boutique hotel.

With the nearby Hope no longer opening for breakfast, the Fox & Anchor is now the only pub in the vicinity of Smithfield to exercise its early morning licence, and over the years it has built up quite a reputation for its full English breakfast. There was a time when early morning customers here would, strictly speaking, have had to be 'lawfully engaged on business in the market', but those days have gone. 'Foxes City Boy breakfast' anyone?

5. THE SUTTON ARMS, No. 6 Carthusian Street, EC1

In 1611, when merchant and political mover and shaker Thomas Sutton bought the ancient Charterhouse for the then not inconsiderable sum of £13,000, he was widely regarded as 'the richest commoner in England'. He promptly set about turning the former monastery complex, which had been established just outside the City walls in 1371 and dissolved in 1537, into a school for boys and also a hospital for 'poor gentleman'. The school was moved to Surrey in 1872; however the hospital evolved into almshouses, which remain here today.

Sutton died in December 1611 but he had clearly left his mark on the area and it seems only fitting that he is remembered by name in not one, but two nearby pubs, of which the Sutton Arms in Carthusian Street is the more notable, architecturally speaking at least.

Carthusian Street itself was laid out in 1699 and the boundary between the City of London and the London Borough of Islington runs directly down its centre. This means that those buildings on the south side are in the City while those on the north, including the Sutton Arms, are technically in Islington.

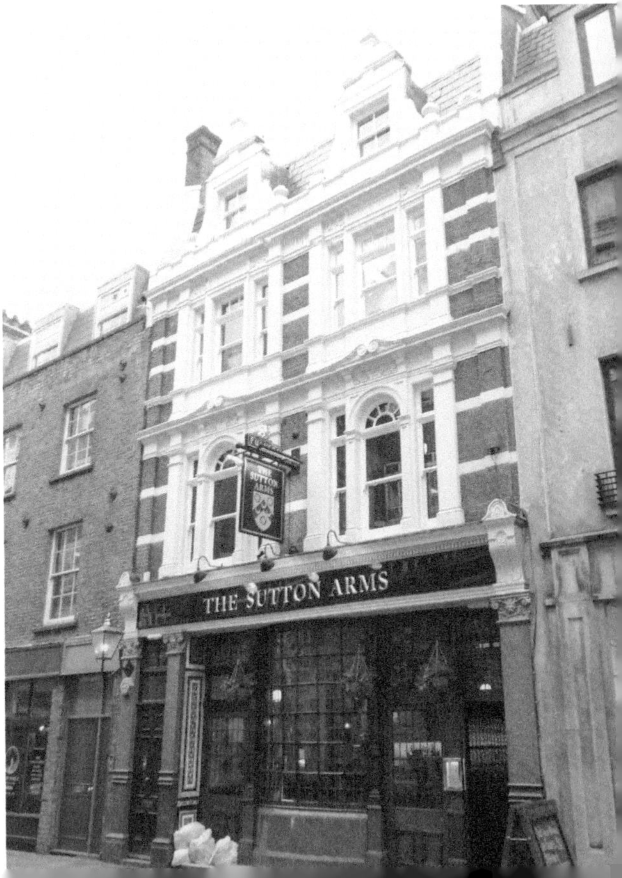

The Sutton Arms, Carthusian Street.

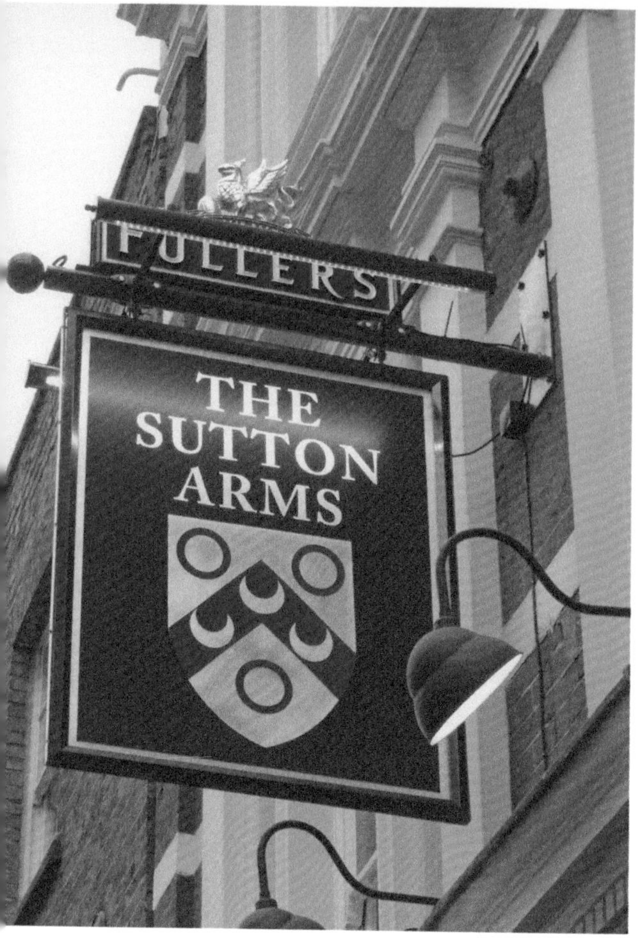

The pub sign features the Sutton family coat of arms.

Notable Exterior

There is a record of the Sutton Arms on this site as early as 1825, but the current rather attractive pub dates from 1898 and was built for the long-defunct New City of London Brewery by the prolific Camberwell firm of Courtney and Fairbairn.

From the outside it looks like a fairly typical London boozer of the late Victorian era, which coincided with the end of the great London pub-building boom. Dark-brown marble pillars and some ornate tiles thankfully survive here, as does a wonderful bow-fronted central window.

Alas a makeover in 2016, by Fuller's of Chiswick, has robbed the interior of almost all of its quirky and slightly scruffy old pub charm, which I suppose is only to be expected from a hostelry that now boasts of offering 'authentic artisanal fare'.

Thankfully a traditional pub sign has been retained and it features the coat of arms of the Sutton family.

6. SUTTON ARMS, No. 16 Great Sutton Street, EC1

This is the second public house in Clerkenwell to call itself the Sutton Arms, but unlike its namesake a short stroll away in Carthusian Street remains a distinctly traditional street corner local in both feel and look, although a growing reputation for cask and craft beer shows it is adapting to the changing pub landscape.

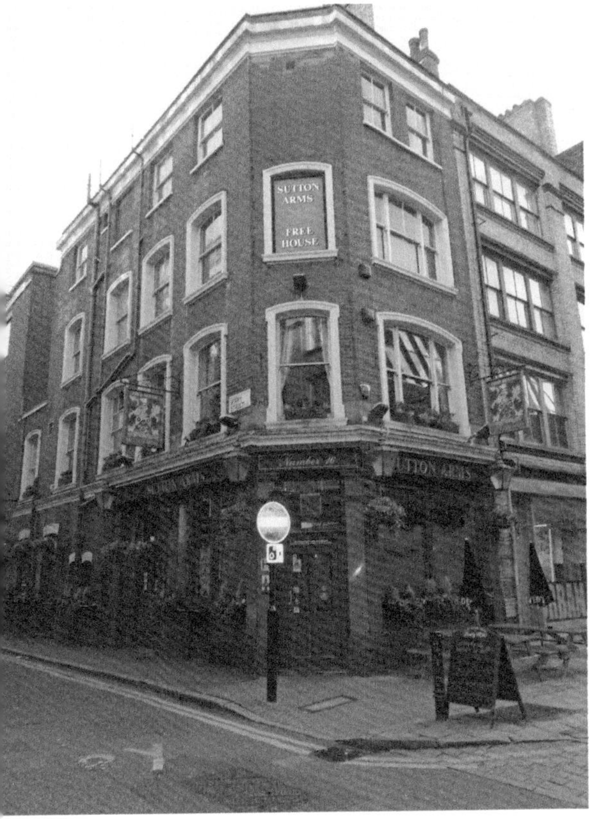

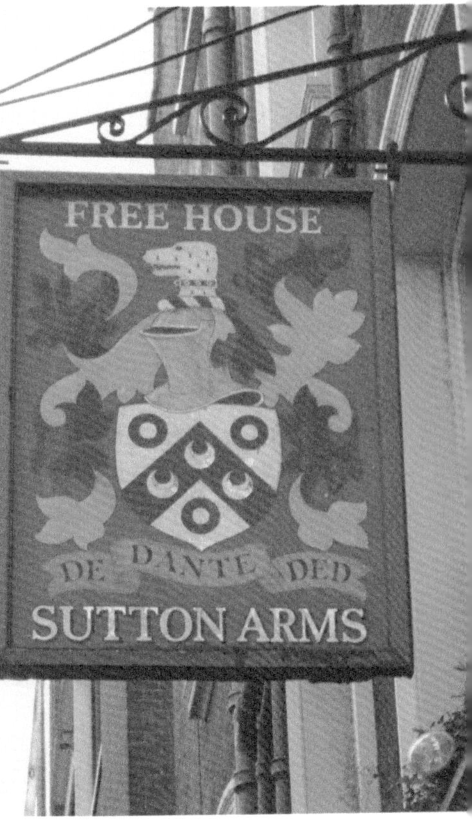

The Sutton Arms, Great Sutton Street.

These days the former printworks and warehouses in the surrounding streets have been largely converted into expensive apartments or 'multifunctional' work spaces, changing the social and cultural feel of the area in the process; but this particular public house is reassuringly old school.

For many years after the Second World War the pub had a full-sized snooker table – a rarity in a London ravaged by bombing. As a result, many professional players were regulars here and there is still a certain raffish charm about the place to this day.

Family Affair

Like its geographically close namesake, the Sutton Arms takes its moniker from Thomas Sutton, who in 1611 acquired the Charterhouse complex of buildings on the edge of the City, which had housed a monastery from 1371 until the dissolution, after which it fell into private ownership. Sutton, reckoned to be one of the wealthiest men in England, founded a boy's school at Charterhouse, which moved to Surrey in 1872, alongside a hospital for distressed 'gentlemen'. The former hospital is now almshouses.

The pub has been run for almost thirty years by Mike Duignan, a local who knows both the area and the pub trade like the back of his hand. His son Jack is also involved these days.

The pattern of streets here are little changed since the 1650s, when they were laid out. There are records of a tavern on this same corner site since at least the 1840s, but the current structure dates from 1897. It is a substantial red-brick affair with three upper floors. Constructed at the height of the great London pub-building boom, compared to some it seems remarkably plain and restrained in execution. Despite which, it is a gem of a boozer in the very heart of Clerkenwell.

7. THE HOPE, No. 94 Cowcross Street, EC1

Smithfield is London's last remaining early morning wholesale market still operating from its original site, where trading has gone on since at least the Middle Ages. While Billingsgate left the City for the Isle of Dogs in 1982 and the famous old fruit and vegetable market at Covent Garden departed to Nine Elms back in 1974, from 2 a.m. each weekday morning you'll still find meat, poultry and game changing hands at Smithfield.

But much has unfortunately changed in recent years, not least that the many public houses in the vicinity that once had early morning licences have either closed for good or instead adopted more conventional hours. Among them is the Hope in Cowcross Street, technically at least in the London Borough of Islington, which as recently as 2016 was still opening its doors at 7 a.m. each weekday morning to cater for those 'lawfully engaged on business in the market'.

It was quite a sight to see ruddy-faced workers from the meat market in bloodied white coats quaffing pints of stout and devouring huge full English breakfasts at a

The Hope's pub sign before and after restoration and refurbishment.

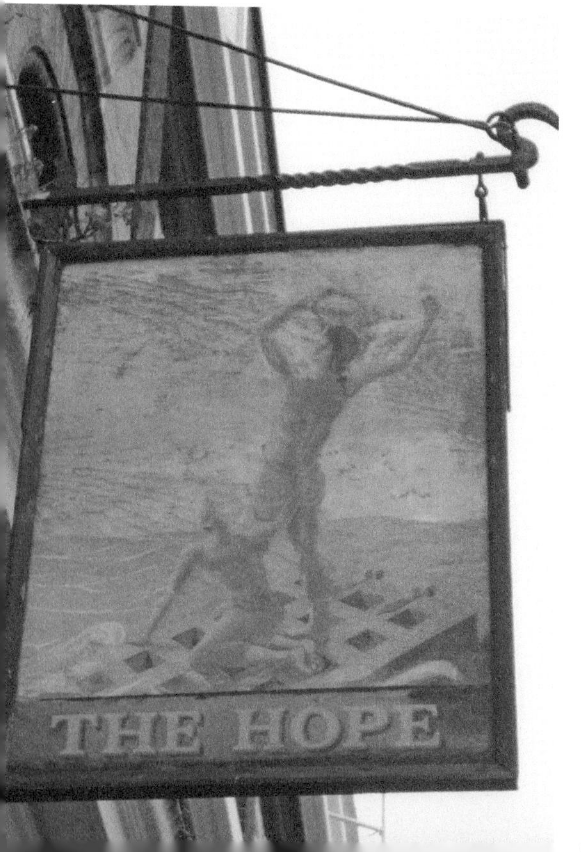

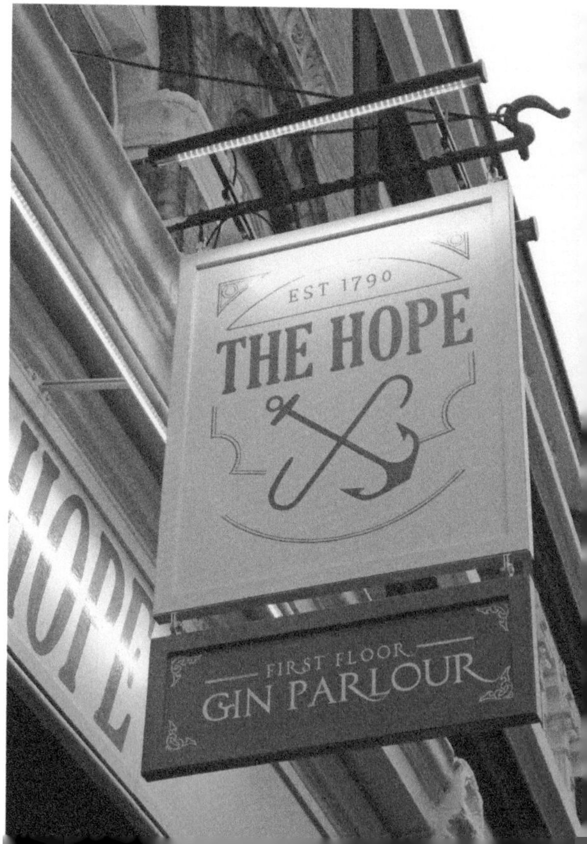

time when most of London is still bleary-eyed and half asleep. These days the pub opens its doors at 11 a.m. and the famous 'Full Monty' is no longer on the menu. You can get pies though.

Renovation

A tavern was first established here in the late eighteenth century and The Hope claims a founding date of 1790. The rather handsome Grade II-listed building you'll encounter today dates from around 1870, the work of the architectural practice of Isaacs and Florence, who were much admired in their day.

The place was given a major spruce up around 1890 when something of a pub-building boom took place, and much of the glorious tiling and etched glass that survives today dates from this refurbishment.

In the spring of 2016 The Hope, which was frankly looking a little sorry for itself, closed for business and darkness descended. The future did not look good for the old place. But I am delighted to report that just in time for Christmas 2016 it reopened courtesy of the Bermondsey Pub Co. after a lengthy and sympathetic renovation and remodel.

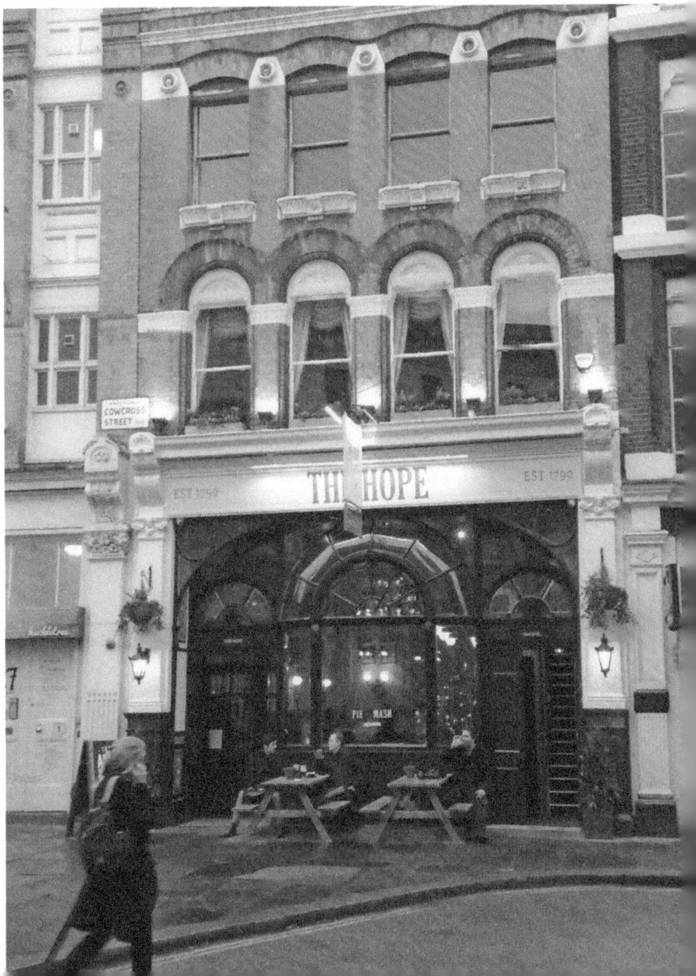

The Hope is one of Smithfield's surviving historic pubs.

So while the rather swish and elegant new-look Hope is far removed from the spit and sawdust market tavern of yesteryear, its historic integrity has been retained and, best of all, it has remained a pub when it could so easily have been turned into a sandwich bar or an artisan coffee shop.

8. THE WHITE BEAR, No. 57 St John Street, EC1

The White Bear doesn't feature in many books about London pubs, which is a great shame. It's a relatively unspoilt and thankfully unpretentious little hostelry, in a part of the capital that has changed dramatically in recent years.

There are records of a pub of this name on this site as early as 1851, but the current red-brick building, five storeys in height with just a single bar, was completed in 1899 having been started the year before. This was a period of recession and uncertainty for London brewers and as a result the building of new public houses had practically ceased.

The White Bear was built by the City of London Brewing Co. in 1899.

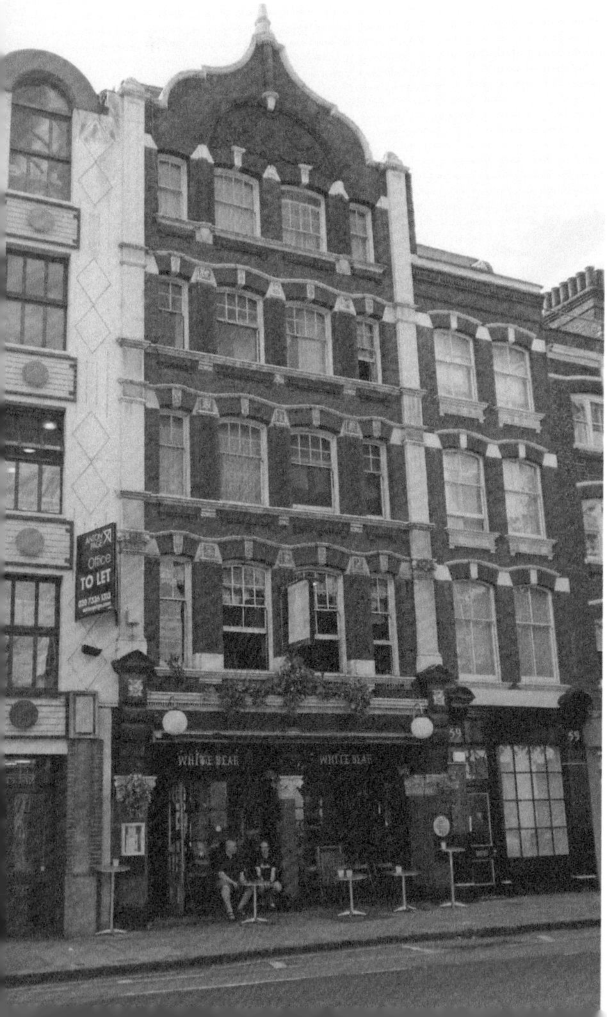

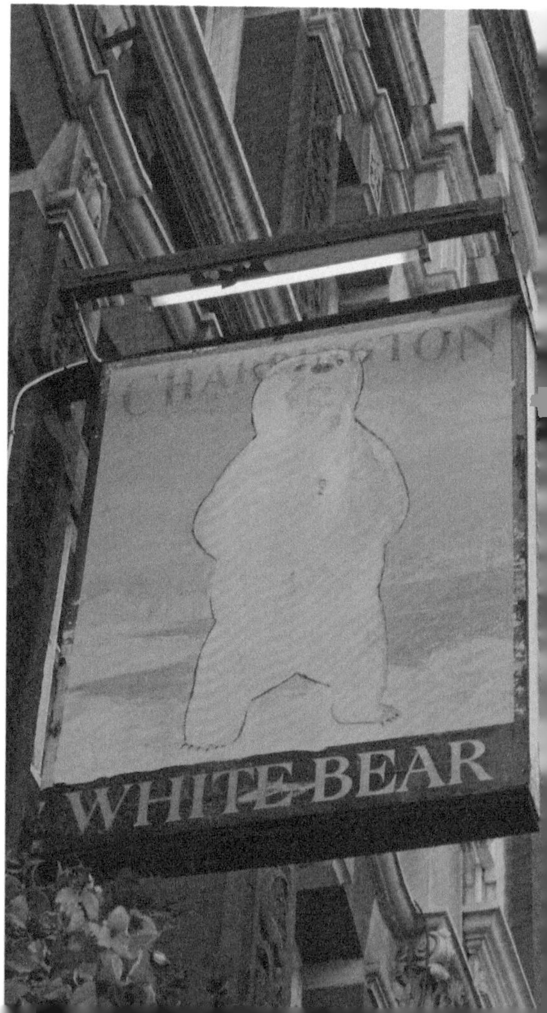

It seems highly likely that because of this the White Bear was built in a somewhat restrained late Victorian style; a functional hostelry with one or two design flourishes to lift the overall feel, most notably some ornate, if rather battered, tiles by the entrance. The original bow window to the front, however, is magnificent.

The pub's name is probably derived from heraldry, as a white bear featured prominently on the coat of arms of several Kentish earls. The current building was constructed for the City of London Brewing Company, then powerful players in the capital's bustling and busy brewing industry.

Historic Brewery

They were notably at the time the only surviving brewer still based in the Square Mile itself, operating from a site in Upper Thames Street (originally just Thames Street before being divided into Lower and Upper stretches) upon which ale had been produced since the early fifteenth century.

The Hour Glass Brewery is recorded at No. 89 Thames Street as early as 1431 and became Calvert's in 1759 when it was acquired by the Calvert family. It became the City of London Brewery Company in 1860, although the old hourglass emblem was retained.

After many centuries, brewing finally ceased as one of the City's heavy industries in 1922 when the Upper Thames Street site terminated production and operations moved to the Swan Brewery in Fulham.

By that time the White Bear was under the ownership of Hoare and Co., of the Red Lion Brewery, Lower East Smithfield, famous for their endearing Toby Jug trademark. When they were taken over by Charrington in 1933, the White Bear became part of their huge London pub estate.

Located just a short stroll from Smithfield Meat Market, today's pub has in some ways the air of a City boozer about it – weekend opening is haphazard – although is actually located in the Borough of Islington.

9. THE JERUSALEM TAVERN, No. 55 Britton Street, EC1

There has been a Jerusalem Tavern in Clerkenwell, in one form or another and with slight variations of name, since at least the seventeenth century, and the current incarnation in Britton Street certainly looks to be of some antiquity. However, despite being housed in a Georgian building of much character and distinction – the sign proclaims 'Anno 1720', although the current frontage dates from 1810 – the pub has only been operating here since 1996.

The earliest version of the pub is recorded in the mid-seventeenth century as the St John of Jerusalem, located roughly where today's Aylesbury Street and Jerusalem Passage meet until it was demolished due to development of the area. It then seems to have moved location several times, for a variety of reasons and with the occasional subtle change of name.

For a time in the 1750s, as the Jerusalem Tavern, it was located in Red Lion Street. There is a nice historical irony in the fact that in 1937 Red Lion Street was renamed Britton Street, in which thoroughfare today's Jerusalem Tavern proudly stands.

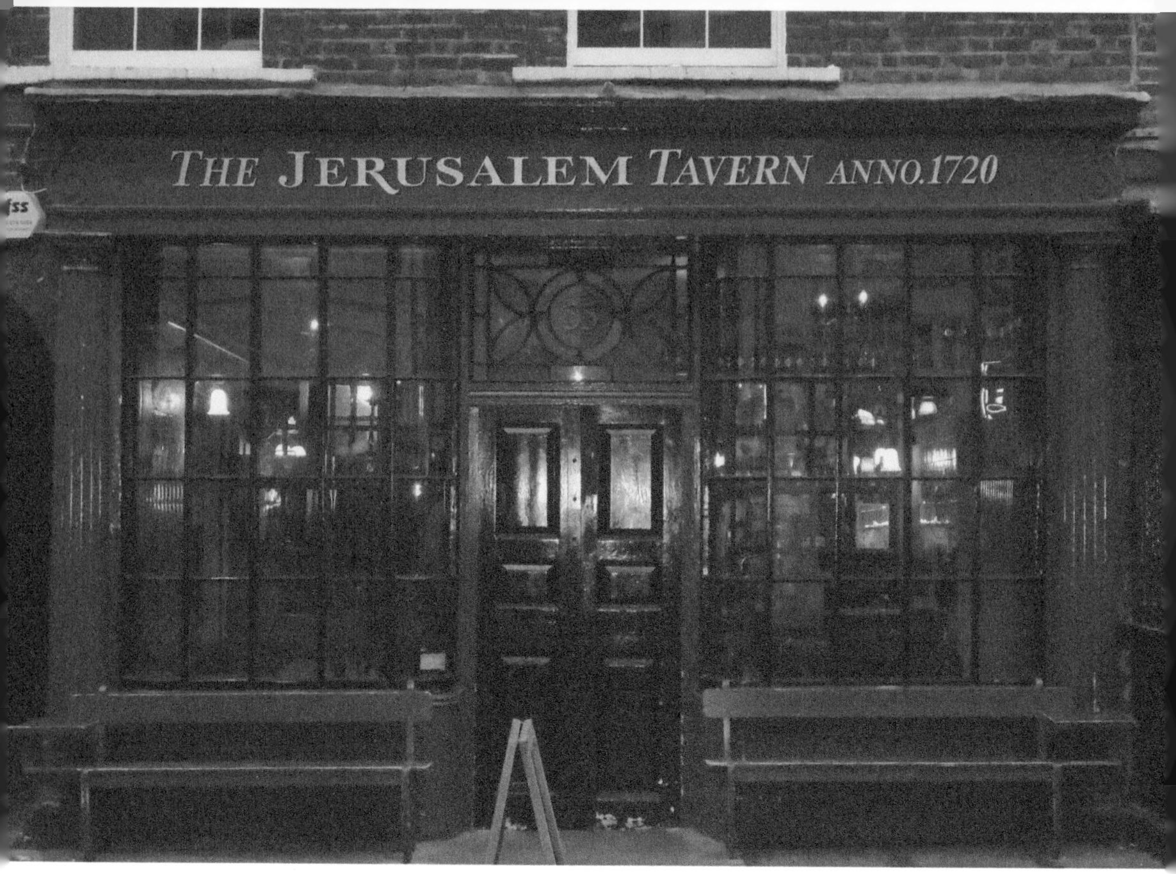

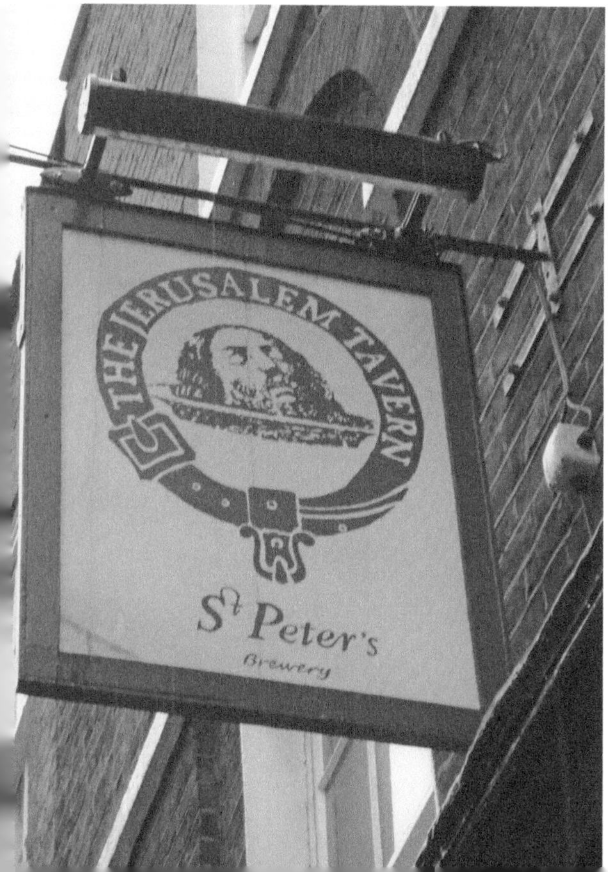

The Jerusalem Tavern, Britton Street.

St John's Gate

To further muddy the historical waters, we also know that from the 1740s onwards there was a tavern operating from inside St John's Gate calling itself, at various times, the Jerusalem Tavern, Old Jerusalem Tavern and the Old Gate. It stayed here until 1876, when it moved just a few yards to occupy a newly built building in St John's Square. That building is still there, at No. 27, although the pub, calling itself by this time the St John's Gate Tavern, closed in 1915.

The name now, as throughout its long history, is inspired by the Priory of St John of Jerusalem, a powerful religious order that once dominated the area. The current Jerusalem Tavern is also the sole London pub of the small St Peter's Brewery, who are based in Suffolk. Despite their modest size they produce a breathtaking range of superb beers.

No. 55 Britton Street was originally a merchant's town house and over the years has housed, variously, a clockmaker's workshop, the offices of a publishing company and an architectural practice. In the early 1990s, as the Jerusalem Coffee House it operated as a recreation of a Georgian coffee house and the wood panelling, pew seating and Delft tiles you see today are from this period. They really do help give the Jerusalem Tavern a magical feel.

On sombre afternoons in winter, with the fire lit and the sound of a ticking clock hanging heavy in the air, a visit to the Jerusalem Tavern is possibly as close as you'll get to stepping back in time to old Clerkenwell. Quite simply, this is an absolutely wonderful pub.

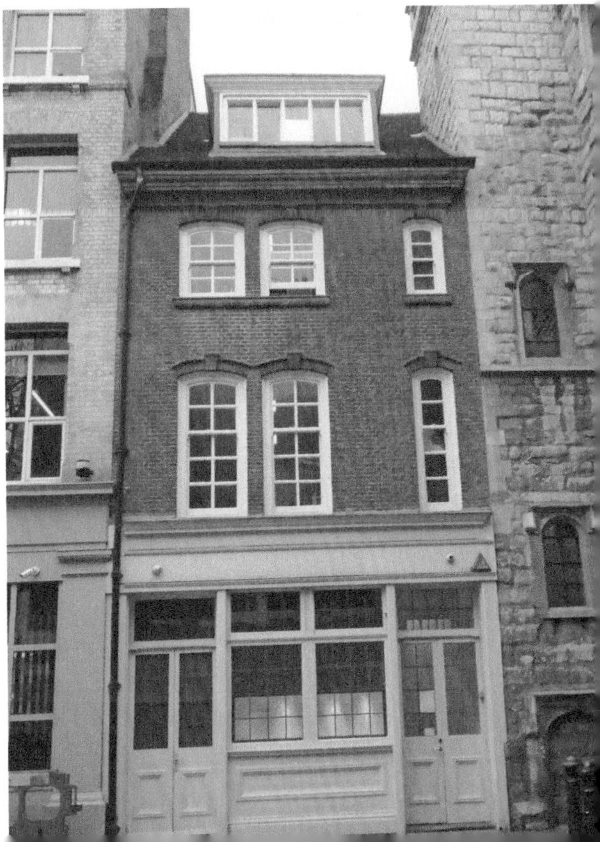

No. 27 St John's Square, formerly the St John's Gate Tavern.

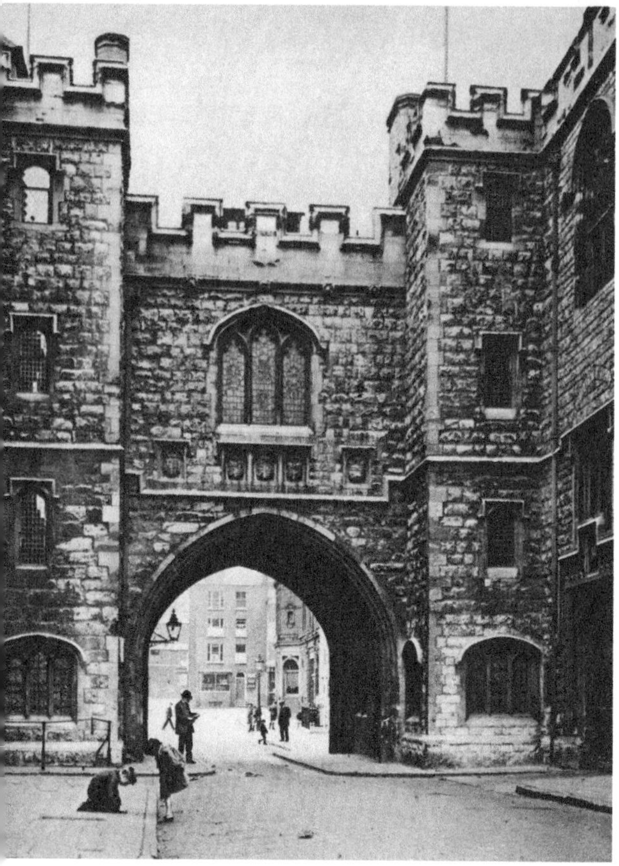

Left: St John's Gate, *c.* 1910, former home of the Jerusalem Tavern.

Below: Today's Jerusalem Tavern was formerly a clockmaker's workshop.

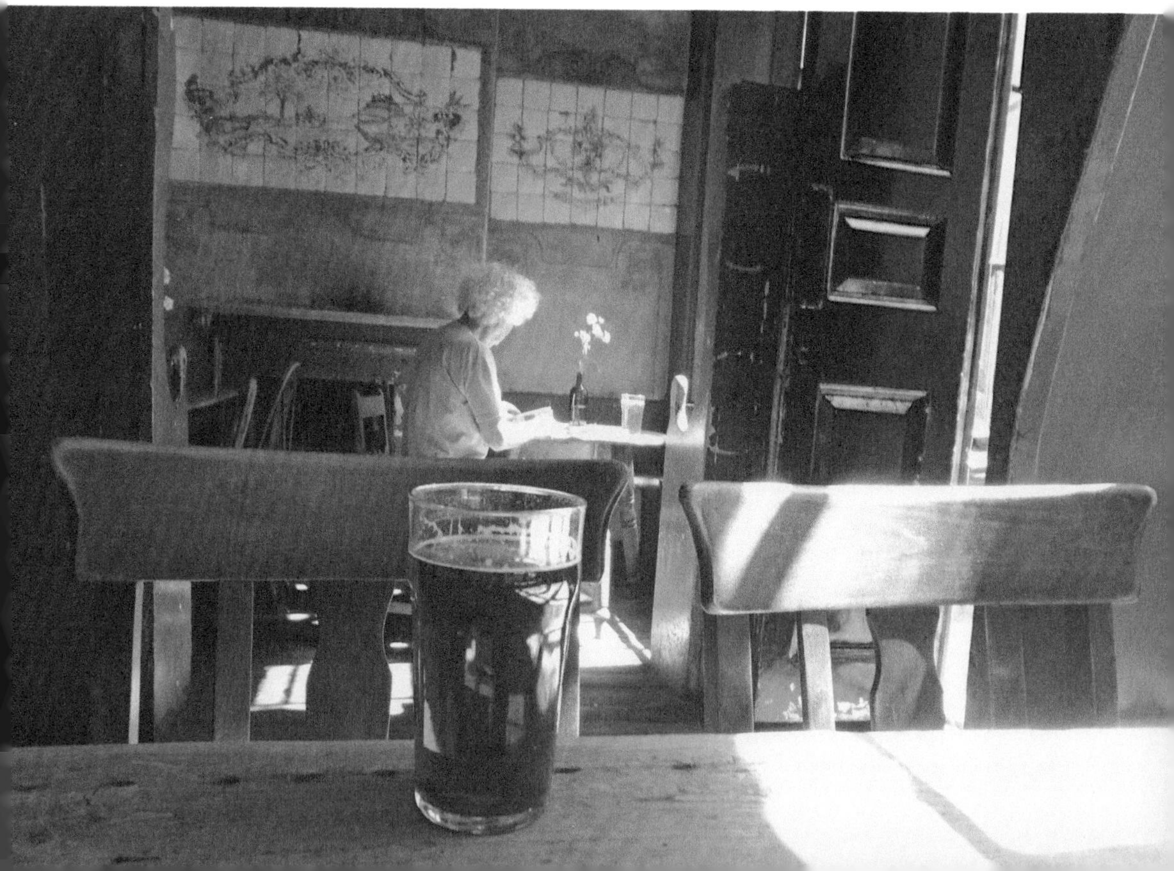

10. THE THREE KINGS, No. 7 Clerkenwell Close, EC1

The gentrification of Clerkenwell continues apace, but there are small pockets of the area that have managed to retain their charm and their feel of genuine antiquity in the face of change, and Clerkenwell Close is most definitely one of them.

Here, standing at a slight curve in the close and opposite the magnificent St James's Church, you'll find The Three Kings, a small pub with a unique atmosphere all of its own.

Records show there has been a pub, with a variety of different names on this site since the mid-eighteenth century. It started out as the Three Johns and became the Oxford Arms around 1783, changing to The Three Kings shortly after. The current structure dates from 1871 and was built for the famous old east London brewer Mann, Crossman and Paulin to a design by architect Robert C. James, although the exquisite green exterior tiles were added in the late 1930s.

The Three Kings, Clerkenwell Close.

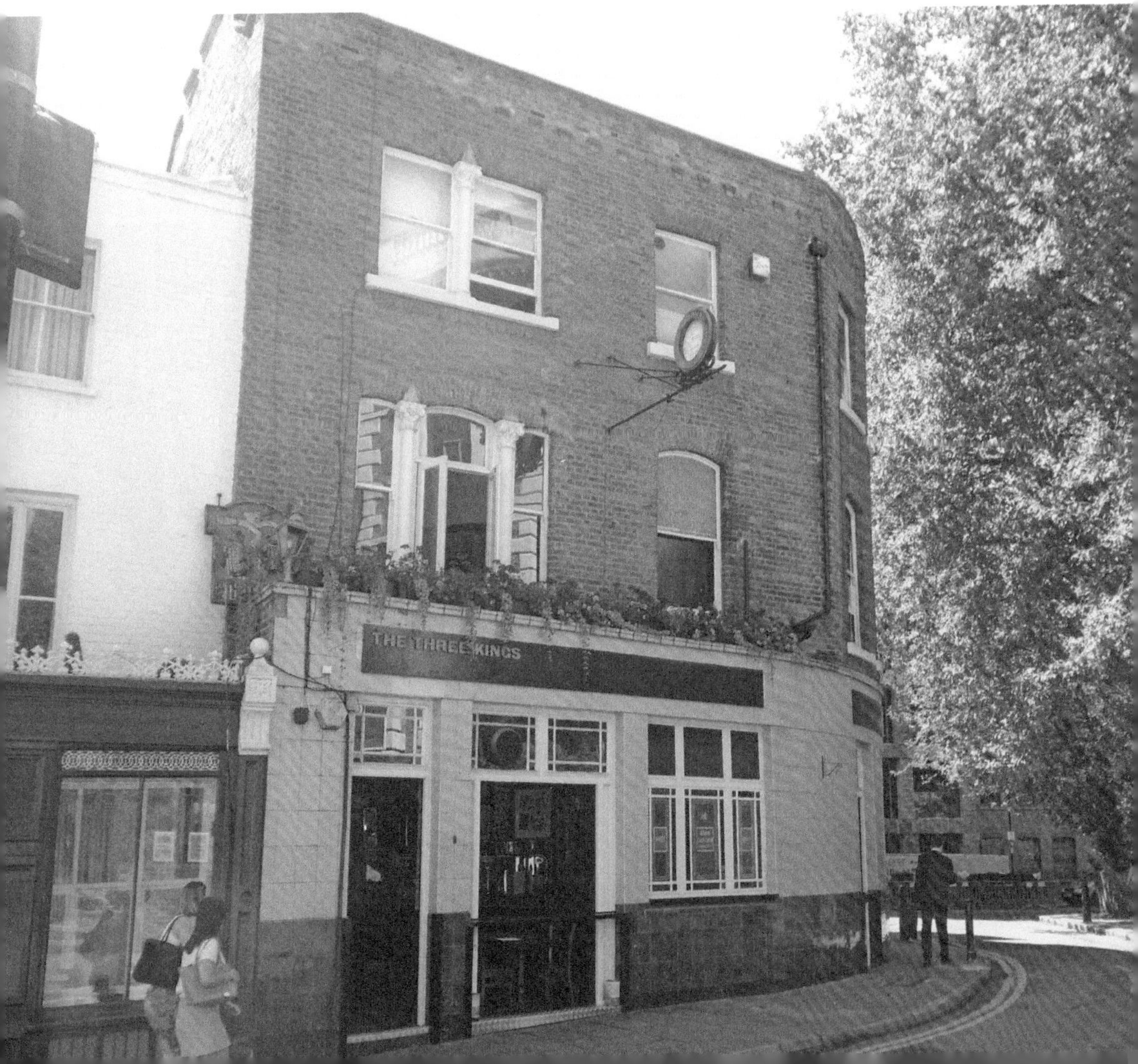

East End Brewer

In 1846 Mann and Sons brewers, based at the famous Albion Brewery in Whitechapel Road, was joined in partnership by Robert Crossman and Thomas Paulin. As Mann, Crossman and Paulin the company went from strength to strength, becoming one of the best known in a congested and competitive London market. Indeed, by the 1880s they were the ninth-largest brewer in Britain.

The company continued to thrive into the twentieth century and enjoyed phenomenal success with its famous Manns Original Brown Ale, first brewed in 1902 and still produced today, although now by Marston's.

In 1958 Mann, Crossman and Paulin merged with Watney, Combe, Reid to form Watney, Mann and brewing only ceased at the Albion Brewery in 1979. The famous Blind Beggar pub, best known through its association with the Kray twins, was for many years the brewery tap.

The exterior of today's Three Kings offers a wonderful visual reminder of this particular chapter in London brewing history. A number of surviving windows from the Mann, Crossman and Paulin years thankfully survive. Prominent on them is the old brewery's famous logo, portraying George slaying the dragon complete with the Latin inscription '*Decus Et Tutamen*' (glory and defence). A later Watney, Combe, Reid sign also survives, post-merger.

John Eichler has run the pub very successfully for many years. His name is enshrined in London rock and roll history for he was in charge at the Hope & Anchor, Upper Street, during that particular pub's transformation into a seminal live music venue.

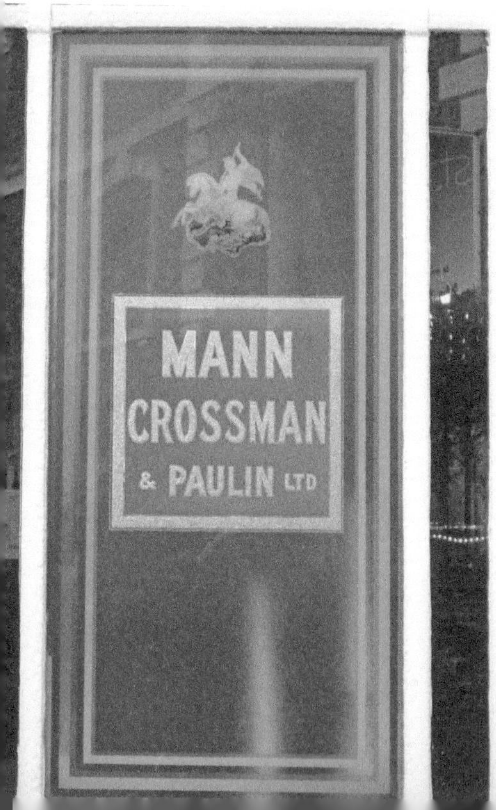

Surviving Mann, Crossman and Paulin window at The Three Kings.

There is, perhaps not surprisingly then, a distinct rock vibe about The Three Kings, where pages from the now sadly defunct music weekly *Melody Maker* are used by way of wallpaper in the ground-floor bar.

11. HORSESHOE, No. 24 Clerkenwell Close, EC1

There is no shortage of artifice or pretence in today's 'newly' fashionable Clerkenwell, but apart from the odd nod to craft beer, The Horseshoe remains a traditional and down to earth London pub with a reassuringly old school atmosphere.

Talking of atmosphere, there is nowhere in London quite like Clerkenwell and there is nowhere in Clerkenwell quite like Clerkenwell Close. It has a truly unique feel to it and on still summer evenings, when near-silence descends, the sense of history is hard to ignore. Part of St Mary's Nunnery stood here and after the Dissolution of the Monasteries a number of grand houses were built, including Newcastle House, which was for many years the London residence of William Cavendish, Duke of Newcastle no less.

Newcastle House was demolished in 1793, although a small turning named Newcastle Row remains as a reminder of sorts. The rich were moving west to newly developed parts of London and Clerkenwell too was changing, now home to many small craft industries and artisan workmen.

The Horseshoe, Clerkenwell Close.

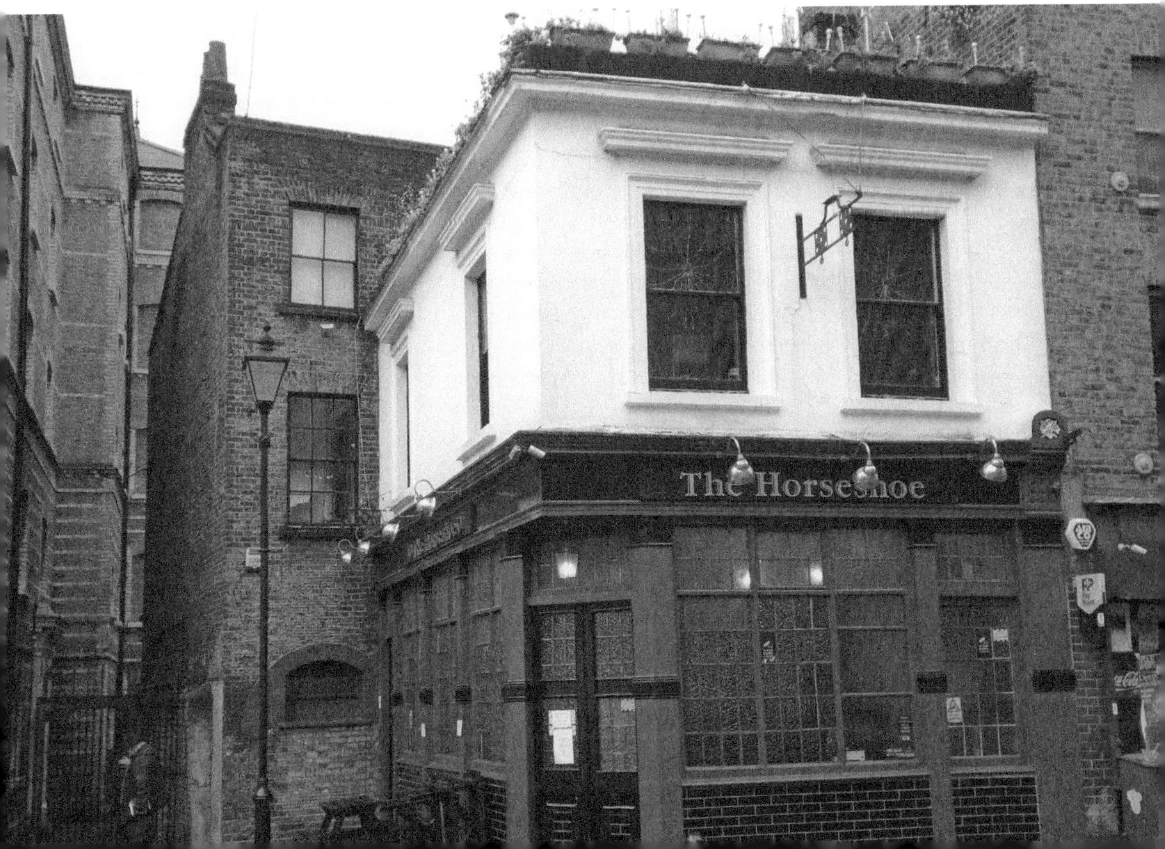

Tunnels

The Horseshoe was trading here as early as 1747 and the current building looks to be late eighteenth-century with a frontage from around 1850. Mary Cosh, mentioning the pub in 1987's *An Historical Walk Through Clerkenwell,* reckoned it had 'the air of a village corner tavern'.

For many years there has been speculation of a tunnel linking the pub with the old Middlesex Sessions House just around the corner in Clerkenwell Green, but no evidence of this has ever been found.

The Horseshoe has certainly seen some changes over the years, including a period in the nineteenth century when it found itself surrounded by slum housing and immense poverty. Today a series of blocks built by the Peabody Trust, founded by the American philanthropist George Peabody in 1862, tower over the pub. They were erected here in 1884, an attempt to alleviate the dreadful conditions prevalent at the time. Alas, despite what appeared to be modest rents of just a few shillings per week, many locally continued to dwell in what Cosh describes as 'stinking courts and alleys'.

From the outside The Horseshoe looks small and modest, but inside is surprisingly spacious. It is also one of London's premier pubs for the noble sport of darts, a fact that very much underlines its old school profile.

The Crown, Clerkenwell Green.

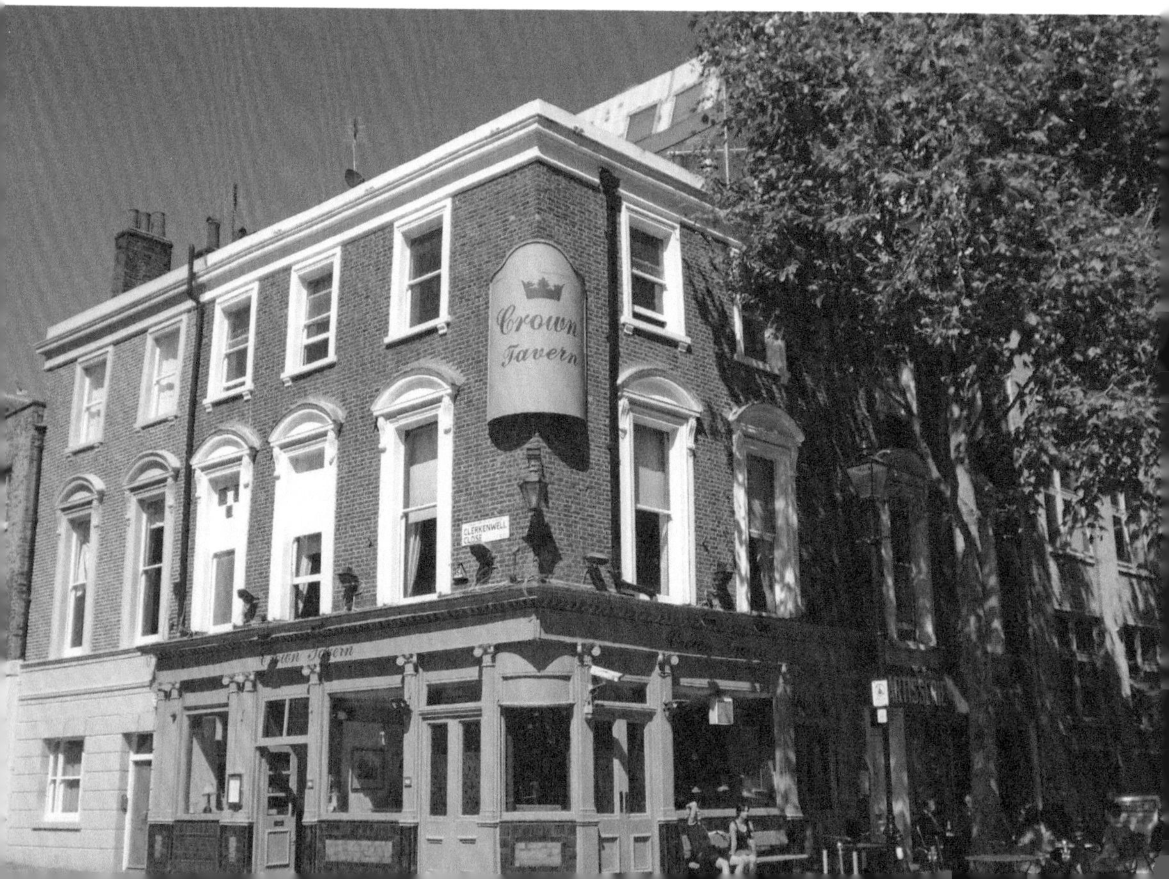

12. THE CROWN, No. 43 Clerkenwell Green, EC1

The Crown remains one of EC1's best-known and enduring public houses. It is wonderfully located in Clerkenwell Green, on the corner with Clerkenwell Close, and despite its current rather corporate feel, has history oozing from its brickwork.

There are records of a pub called the Crown, briefly the Crown and Anchor, on this site as early as 1641. For many years it was nicknamed the Clockhouse, a reference to the many regulars who were employed in the local watch and clock industry, of which Clerkenwell was once a centre.

To tie in with this, the Crown was once renowned for a vast collection of timepieces, although with one notable exception these have sadly disappeared. The surviving clock in question sits in the pub's back room, a rather grand black-lacquered affair that claims to have hung at Rye House, Hertfordshire, supposedly the location in 1683 where a Whig plan to assassinate Charles II was drawn up.

More than 300 years on historians remain divided on just how serious the so-called Rye House Plot actually was, while there is no hard evidence to validate the claim, made in gold lettering on the case, that this was indeed 'Ye Conspiritors clock'. It is clearly, whatever its true provenance, very old. It's a shame the hands are now missing.

Lenin and Trotsky

The current Crown dates from 1815, with some reworking around 1860 according to Pevsner in *The Buildings of England*. For much of the nineteenth century it was a popular venue for grand dances and concerts. These were held in the upstairs Apollo Room and a framed ticket from 1896 boasts of 'A Grand Bohemian Concert' to 'benefit' the widow of Thomas Byford. Byford had died suddenly without leaving any provision for his wife.

It is perhaps hard to believe now, given the surrounding gentrification, but Clerkenwell was once a hotbed of radicalism. The Marx Memorial Library is still located only a few yards from the Crown while the Green itself was, and still occasionally is, the starting point for political demonstrations. It's also where Dickens has the Artful Dodger try to teach Oliver Twist the not-so-noble art of stealing handkerchiefs.

A claim made in some quarters is that Lenin and Trotsky, both exiled in London, met at the Crown to talk revolution, or possibly football. Once again, there is no hard evidence to back this claim up – although I'm sure both men liked a pint from time to time. Revolution, undoubtedly, can be thirsty work.

13. BETSEY TROTWOOD, No. 56 Farringdon Road, EC1

On first impression the Betsey Trotwood doesn't seem a particularly remarkable pub. Standing at the junction of Farringdon Road and Farringdon Lane, architecturally it is a pretty standard Victorian hostelry of its day, built in 1874/75. But venture inside, order a drink and then wait for the rumble.

You see the Betsey, as it is affectionately known locally, is located almost directly above the Metropolitan line as it thunders to and from nearby Farringdon station. Now the Metropolitan line isn't just any old London Underground line; it is

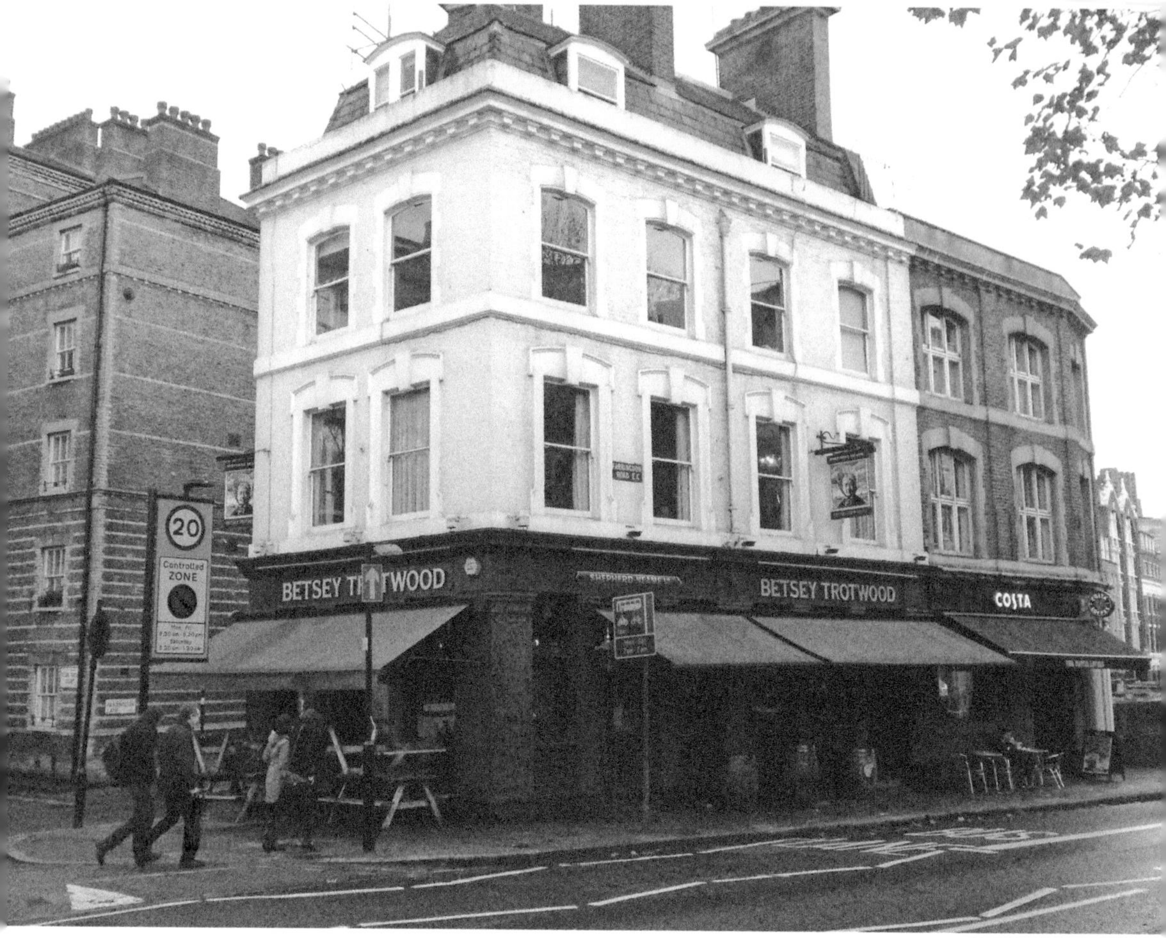

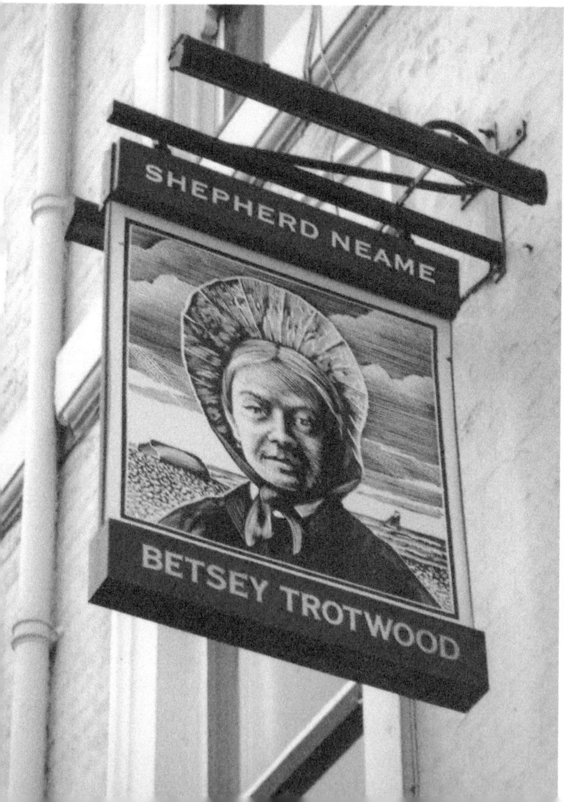

The Betsey Trotwood, Farringdon Road.

London's first Underground line. Indeed, it is the world's very first Underground line, opened on January 10 1863, and initially running from the aforementioned Farringdon station to Paddington.

From King's Cross to Farringdon the line roughly follows the route of the Fleet, perhaps London's most famous 'lost' river. Construction of the line was a huge job that caused major change to both the local landscape and the local community. There was much demolition and destruction, but there was also much new construction, including the pub we know today as the Betsey Trotwood.

Charles Dickens

There had been a pub on, or very close to, this site prior to the arrival of the underground railway. Records show that a hostelry called the Butcher's Arms was located at Pear Tree Court, which runs off Farringdon Lane and is barely 10 yards from the Betsey.

Pear Tree Court is an unassuming and narrow thoroughfare, and very atmospheric with it. Its close proximity might help explain why, in 1983, the Butcher's Arms changed its name. Betsey Trotwood is, of course, a character from Charles Dickens's *David Copperfield* and as touched upon elsewhere in this book, the great writer knew Clerkenwell and its environs intimately. Pear Tree Court, it is widely accepted, features in *Oliver Twist* as the 'narrow court' that the Artful Dodger and Oliver traverse en route to Clerkenwell Green. It is here, of course, where the Dodger's attempts to teach Oliver the pickpocket's art go disastrously wrong.

For many years the rather brutalist offices of *The Guardian* newspaper stood opposite the Betsey, but this has now been obliterated from the landscape following the newspaper's move in 2008 to new premises near King's Cross. The Betsey, however, remains a popular pub with those working in the media and has also carved out a reputation for itself as a live music venue. For many years it has been owned by Kent brewer Shepherd Neame, the oldest in the country.

14. THE CASTLE, Nos 34–35 Cowcross Street, EC1

The Castle is unique among English pubs in so far as it is the only one to hold a pawnbroker's licence. This means, in theory at least, that you can pop in with Uncle Burt's ruby cufflinks or that old Ming vase that Auntie Madge left you, and the pub's landlord, if the fancy takes them, can give you cash against said items.

This strange situation stems from an incident that, so London lore has it, took place at this venerable old tavern sometime around 1820. George IV, who if the date is correct had only recently taken the throne following the death of his father, had been attending a cockfight at the nearby Hockley-in-the-Hole, one of London's most notorious districts and the resort of thieves, pickpockets, highwaymen and prostitutes.

George, an inveterate and by all accounts not very successful gambler, found himself without ready cash to hand and so made his way to the nearby Castle where after some negotiation he persuaded the landlord to give him a cash advance against his gold watch. Apparently the landlord was unaware of George's real identity.

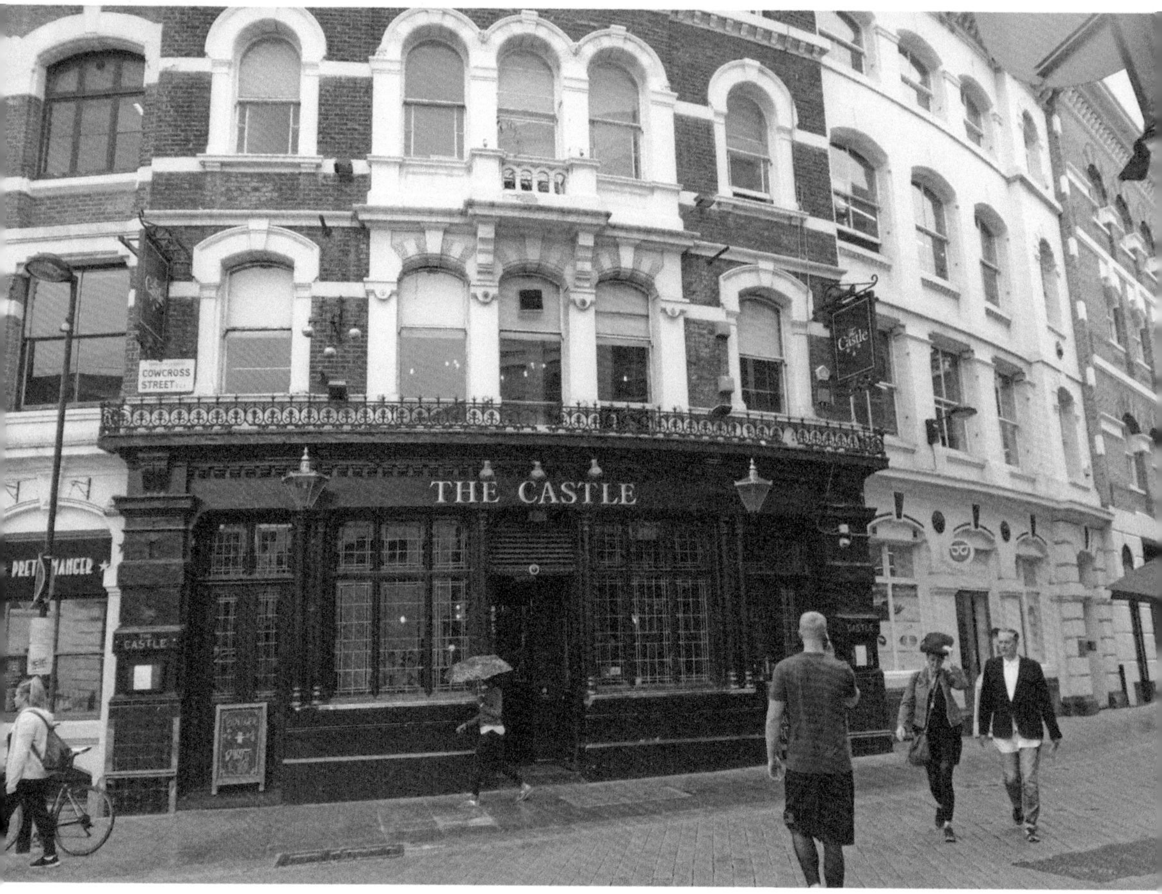

The Castle, Cowcross Street.

Three Balls

Returning to the cockfight with his newly acquired funds, George enjoyed a winning streak and, the following morning, a royal flunky was despatched to the Castle to redeem the gold watch and to present the no doubt puzzled landlord with a pawnbroker's licence. The sign of the three pawnbrokers' balls still hang outside the pub.

Today's Castle is an attractive Grade II-listed building, elegantly curved on the corner of Cowcross Street and Turnmill Street, which opened for business in 1867 and was designed by architect H. Dawson. However a pub of the same name has occupied the same site since the late eighteenth century.

Clerkenwell today is one of London's most fashionable quarters, but for much of the eighteenth and nineteenth centuries the area around Turnmill Street was a notorious rookery and as late as 1867 the *City Press* was describing the Castle as a place frequented by 'the knackers and bone pickers of the metropolis'. You're more likely these days to mingle with media types.

Like a lot of old pubs in Clerkenwell, the Castle has been given something of an interior update, but a wonderful old Bass and Co. mirror has survived, as has a striking, if perhaps aesthetically challenging, oil painting that takes up a large part of the back wall and imagines the famous pawnbroking incident of 1864. It bears the enigmatic inscription 'Bruce 1964'.

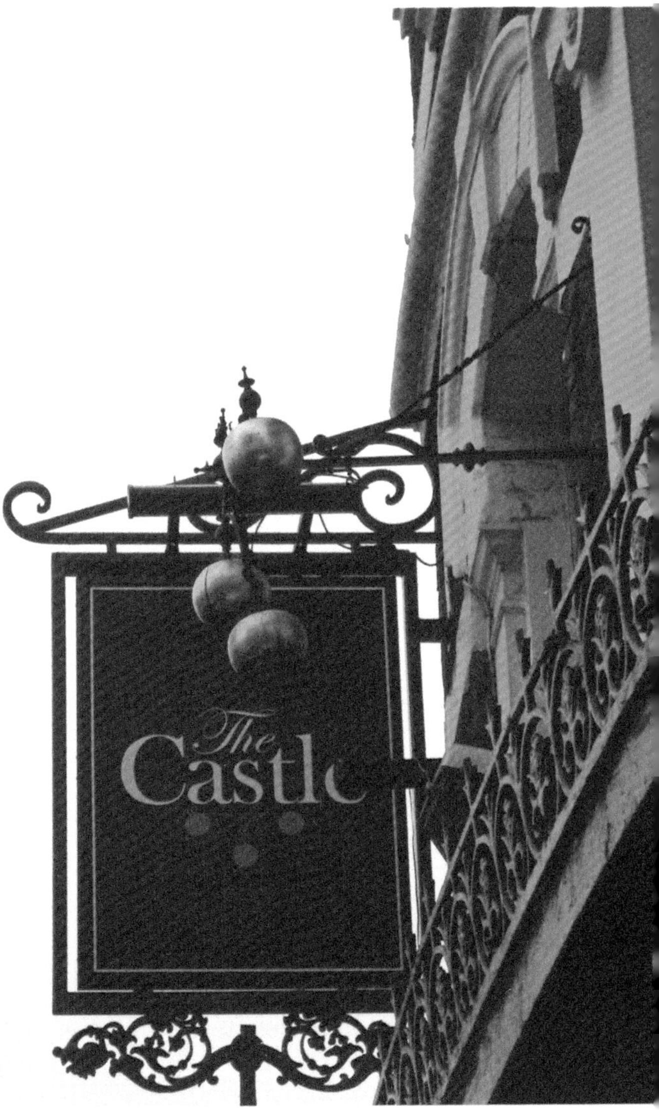

The Castle's pub sign, complete with three pawnbrokers' balls.

15. THREE COMPASSES, No. 66 Cowcross Street, EC1

Cowcross Street is today at the heart of fashionable Clerkenwell, a thoroughfare of restaurants, cafés and swanky media and architects offices. But until the mid-nineteenth century it was at the centre of one of London's most notorious rookeries, a place of low men and fallen women, of horse thieves and pickpockets and worse.

During this time there was a plethora of pubs in the neighbourhood, and although many have disappeared, a few of some antiquity, such as the Three Compasses, are still with us.

Indeed the founding date of 1723 is proudly displayed on today's pub sign, although the pub itself has been rebuilt several times since and the current structure looks to be post-war, if perhaps a little earlier. It was originally known as simply the Compasses.

Back in its early days, like every watering hole in the neighbourhood, a large criminal element would have featured among the pub's clientele, but few taverns could boast a criminal as actual landlord.

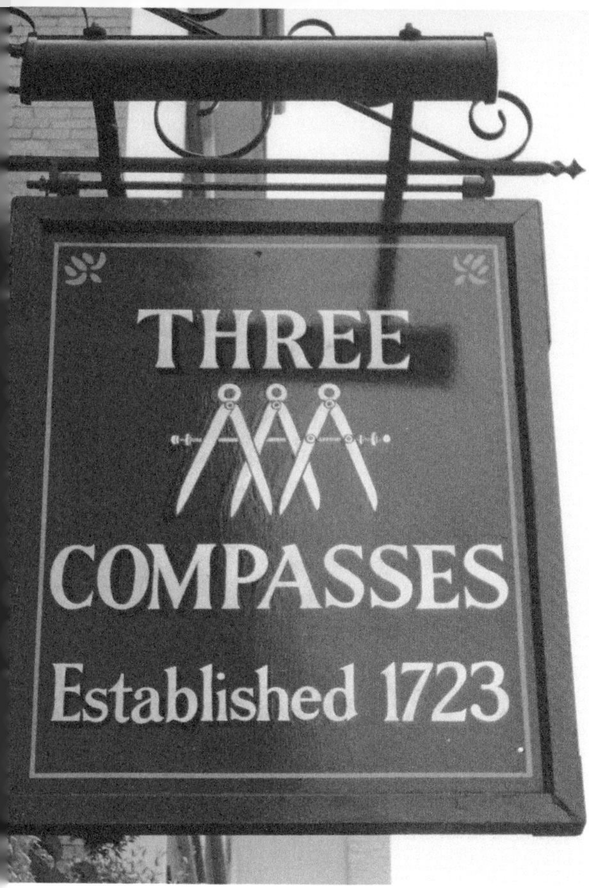

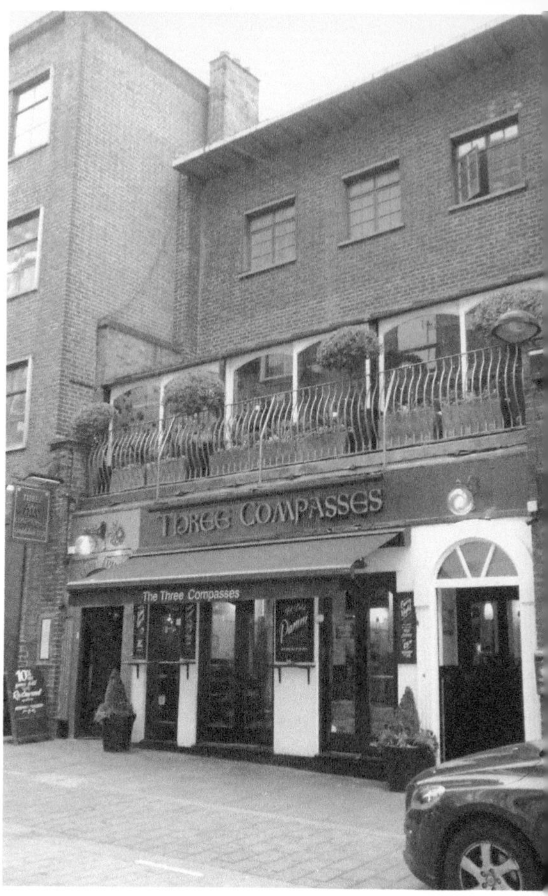

The Three Compasses has traded in Cowcross Street since 1723.

Landlord Highwayman

William Lancaster ran the Compasses during the late eighteenth century, but in 1796 it emerged that he was leading something of a double life, and when he wasn't pulling pints he was riding out as a highwayman. Some sources even suggest he was among the infamous Hounslow highwaymen, who preyed on those travelling in and out of London to the west.

Lancaster met a grisly end the following year, as the *Oxford Journal* of 1797 reported. The Earl of Strathmore was on his way from London to Scotland when near Finchley Common his carriage was held up by two masked men.

One of the men attempted to fire his pistol into the carriage but it did not go off. The Earl, no doubt as a precaution against robbery, had a blunderbuss in the carriage with him and promptly fired, hitting one of the two assailants, blasting him off his steed and in all likelihood killing him instantly. The felled robber was William Lancaster, who only days earlier had been freed from prison after a charge against him of robbing Lord Boringdon had been dropped through lack of evidence. Some people never learn.

Today's Three Compasses is more traditional than many pubs in this neck of the woods and is resolutely felon free.

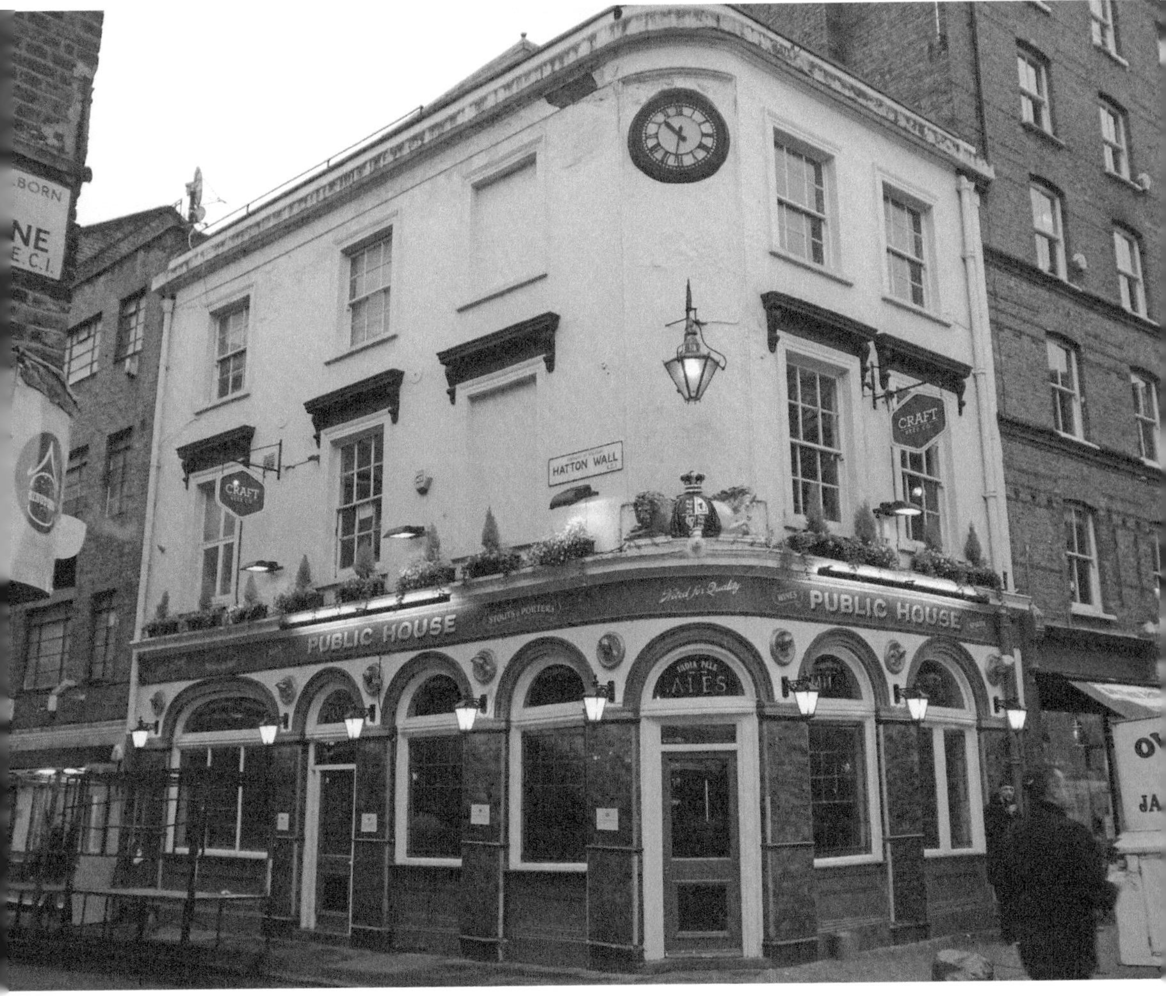

The Craft Beer Co., Leather Lane.

16. THE CRAFT BEER CO., No. 82 Leather Lane, EC1

Amid all the gloom and doom of pub closures and pub conversions there is the odd bit of good news, such as the story behind the Craft Beer Co. in Leather Lane.

This lovely old pub on the corner of Leather Lane and Hatton Wall was formerly known to generations of locals and market traders as the Clock House, a name it adopted in the 1860s. The name was no doubt inspired by the many watch and clockmakers and repairers who worked in the streets surrounding nearby Hatton Garden. The pub was originally known as the Coach and Horses, first opening here in 1785.

The Clock House, from personal memory, was a slightly scruffy and determinedly no thrills boozer, busy with market folk during the day and locals from the nearby Bourne Estate at other times.

Its otherwise rather dull interior was notable for a magnificent mirrored ceiling, divided into twelve distinct parts in the pattern of a clock. It's still there today and well worth craning your neck for.

Changing Times

There has been a market in Leather Lane for centuries, and the thoroughfare is mentioned in John Stow's famous survey of 1598. For many years it was a bustling London street market specialising in clothes and household goods. In recent years, however, the emphasis has moved almost entirely to street food aimed at lunchtime workers.

This part of town has changed dramatically in recent years and has become very fashionable. That change was reflected in 2011 when the Clock House was transformed into the Craft Beer Co. Founded by Martin Hayes to 'celebrate old school British pub values, alongside the very best in modern standards and service', this Mecca to both craft and cask beer was an instant success and several other Craft Beer Co. pubs have opened since.

If you are even remotely interested in beer then this is a place you should visit. On a recent visit I counted an incredible sixteen cask ale/ciders on offer and twenty-one keg offerings, in addition to a mind-boggling range of bottled beers from all over the world that included Belgian sours and lambics. They even have a handful of barley wines.

It is today an undeniably hip place to sip your saison, but also, I am delighted to report, retains some of its original charm. In addition to the aforementioned ceiling, a stunning mirror advertising 'Charrington's Celebrated Burton Ales' has survived the makeover. It seems to encapsulate this near perfect fusion of the past and what would appear to be the future.

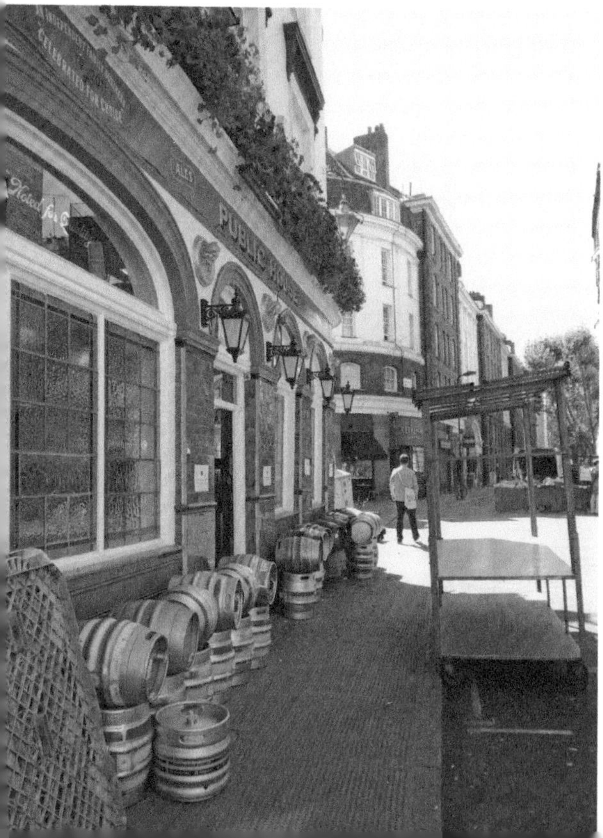

The Craft Beer Co. has become a Mecca for beer lovers.

17. THE HAT AND TUN, No. 3 Hatton Wall, EC1

On one wall towards the rear of The Hat and Tun, a handsome old pub tucked away just off busy Clerkenwell Road, is a picture of Sir Christopher Hatton, one of the most powerful and influential movers and shakers of the Elizabethan age. This seems apt considering he gave his name to the surrounding area, Hatton Garden, and also to Hatton Wall, which is the address you'll need to give the black cab driver if you want to visit this pub.

Sir Christopher Hatton was a courtier, politician and, so legend has it, one-time lover of Elizabeth I. She was certainly very fond of him, for a while at least, and it was at her instigation that he was allowed to develop and live on a large piece of land that the poor old Bishops of Ely were 'persuaded' to lease to him. He was made Lord Chancellor in 1587.

Despite enjoying vast wealth for much of his life, he died with heavy debts. Apparently Elizabeth visited him just nine days before his death. Some sources claim she personally fed him broth.

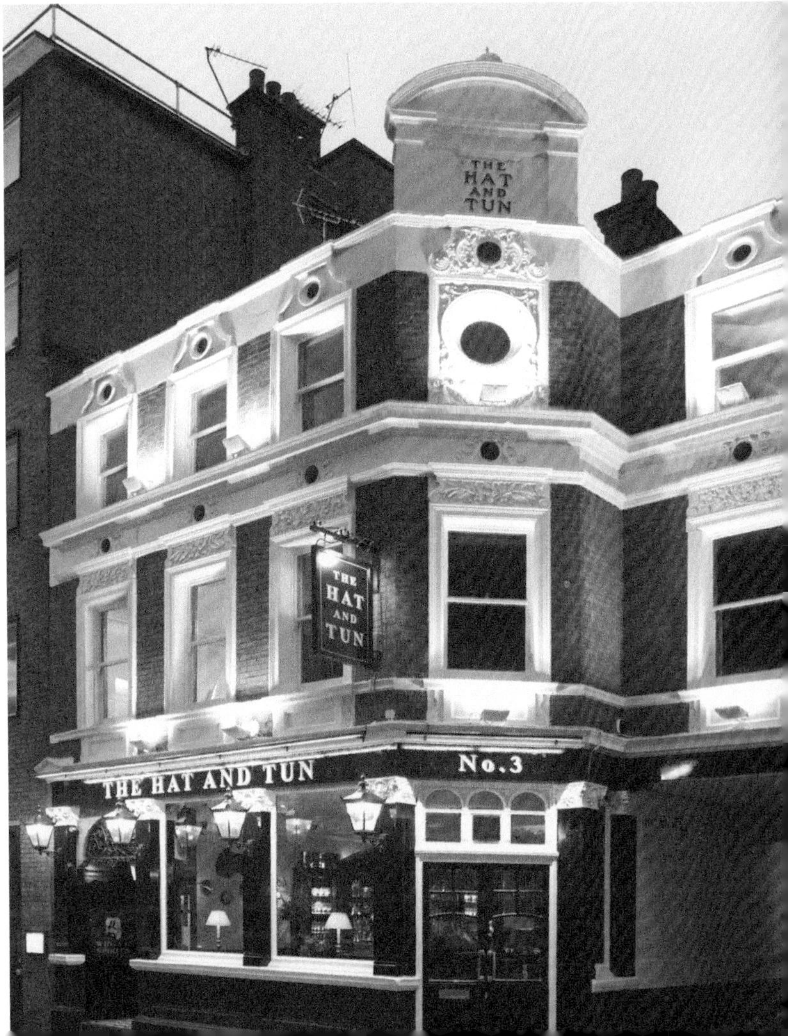

The Hat and Tun,
Hatton Wall.

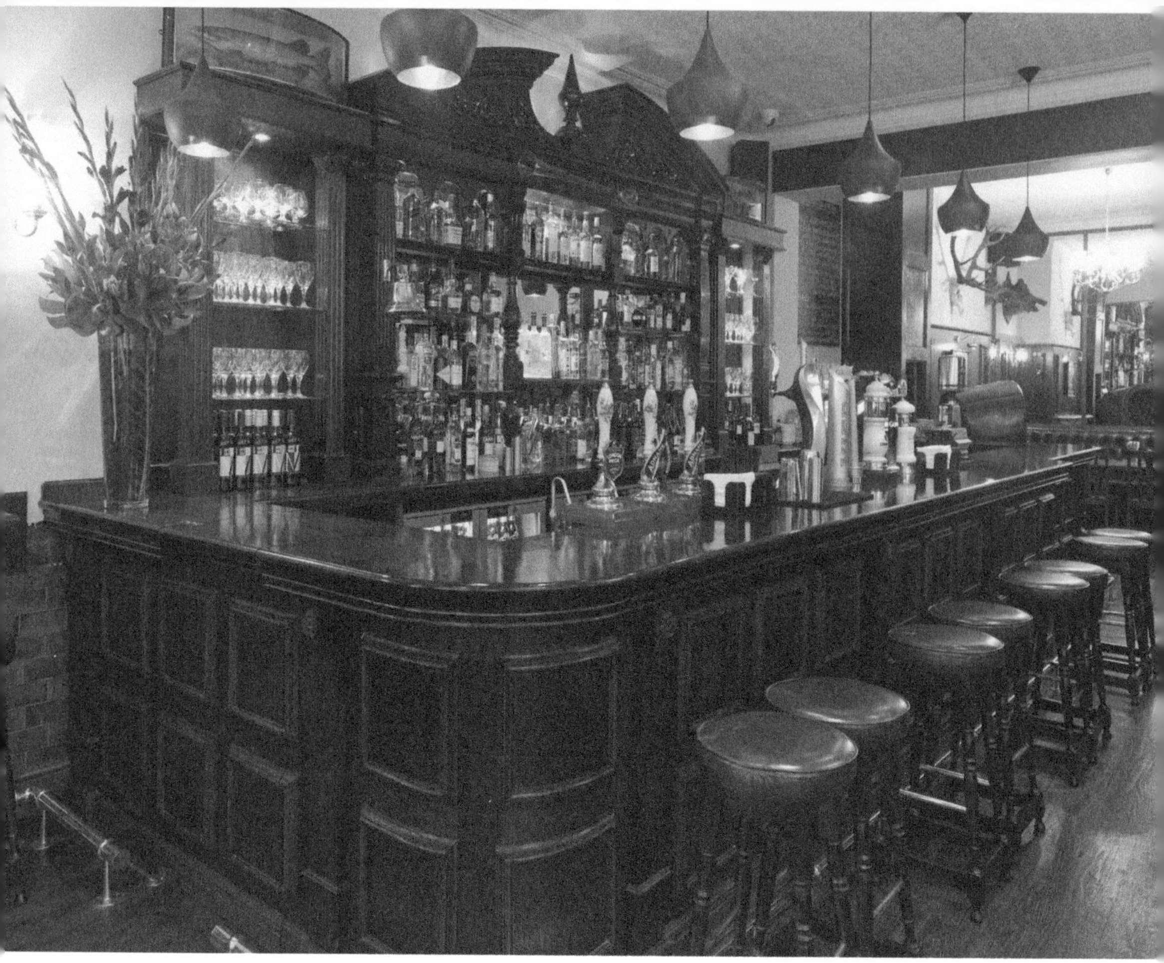

The Hat and Tun, Hatton Wall.

Toff Motif

Today's Hat and Tun manages to combine a lovely old traditional interior, a veritable riot of wooden panelling, with a contemporary gastropub-lite feel. I would guess the current building is late Victorian, and the beautiful bar back early twentieth century. The many stuffed animal heads adorning the walls, however, are a mystery.

A nice surviving feature can be seen in a recessed area as you enter the pub, namely a polychromatic glass panel featuring a character that the Brewery History Society in their Defunct Brewery Livery index refer to as the 'Charrington toff motif'.

In the year 2000 the pub changed its name to Deux Beers, which if you say it really quickly sounds an awful lot like De Beers, the international diamond dealers who for many years were based on the fringes of Hatton Garden. I prefer Hat and Tun myself, which has thankfully been restored, and is in itself a play on Sir Christopher's surname.

18. GUNMAKERS, No. 13 Eyre Street Hill, EC1

Clerkenwell today is awash with loft style apartments, swanky restaurants and media and design offices, but you don't have to step too far off the beaten track to discover remnants of the area's industrial past.

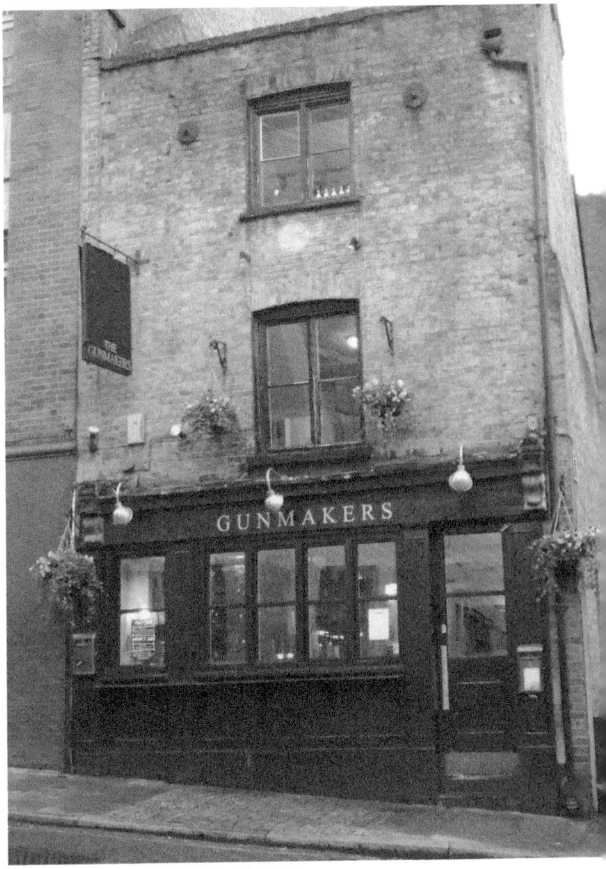

Gunmakers, Eyre Street Hill.

Take Eyre Street Hill for instance, which meanders from busy Clerkenwell Road down to Warner Street. Here the surrounding buildings provide rather imposing architectural evidence of the printing and manufacturing activity that once dominated around these parts. There's even an electricity sub-station for good measure. You will also discover the Gunmakers public house, which has a story of its own to tell.

The Gunmakers stands as part of a terrace development that was clearly interrupted by Second World War bombing. There are certainly records of a tavern on this site as early as 1848, although there are conflicting accounts of where the name comes from. One version suggests the Gunmakers is named after a nearby workshop where rifles were manufactured. Another version suggests the name was inspired by the pub's close proximity to the location, now marked by a blue plaque in nearby Hatton Garden, where Hiram Maxim invented the machine gun. However that wasn't until 1881, by which time the Gunmakers Arms, to give the pub its former full name, was already established.

Little Italy

Eyre Street Hill was for many years at the heart of London's 'Little Italy'. Italians started to make their presence felt in this part of Clerkenwell in the 1770s, but it was throughout the nineteenth century that they really stamped their mark on the area.

Certainly a look at the list of publicans who have run the Gunmakers over the years makes for illuminating reading. 'Guvnors' listed in the early 1800s include such doughty British names as Charles Cole, John Hall and James Bingham.

However by 1882 Rocco Rabboni is at the helm and in the ensuing years the likes of Giacomo Camoccio, Paolo Beschizza and the Cattini family are all associated with the pub.

Since the 1960s the once thriving Italian community has dispersed all over London, but there are many remaining traces of the area's past and one of them can be still be seen just a few yards from the Gunmakers – namely the premises of Chiappa Ltd, 'organ builders'. Founded by Giuseppe Chiappa, the company have been in Eyre Street Hill since 1877 and are still trading.

As for the Gunmakers, these days it has a distinctly gastropub feel to it and looks rather swish in the modern Clerkenwell way.

19. THE EAGLE, No. 159 Farringdon Road, EC1

For most of its existence The Eagle, an attractive but unassuming pub, was a typical Clerkenwell boozer catering for thirsty postal workers from nearby Mount Pleasant sorting office and working-class locals, of which there were once many living in nearby 'model dwellings' such as Corporation Buildings and Farringdon Road Buildings, both sadly now demolished.

But in January 1991 everything changed as The Eagle took the lead in what can only be described as both a gastronomic and – looking at the bigger picture – cultural

The Eagle can claim to be London's first gastropub.

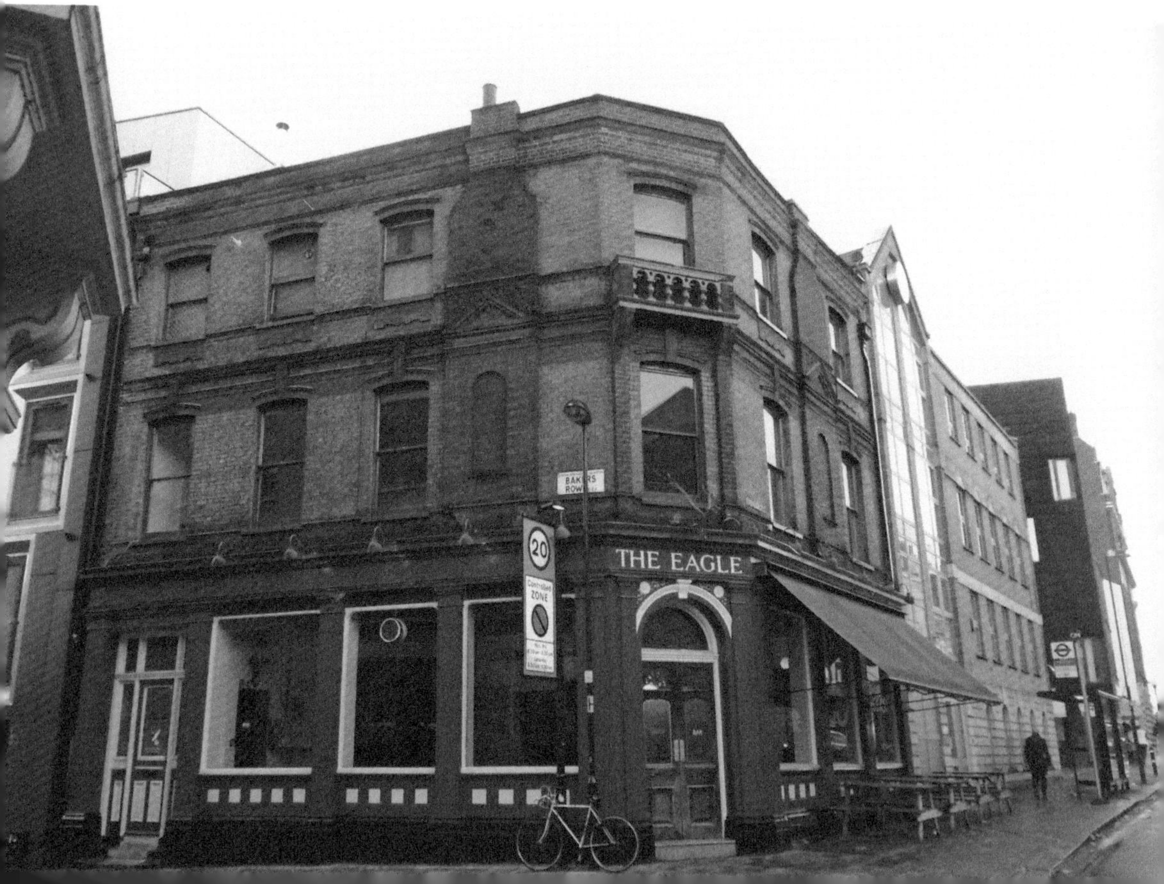

revolution. Debate still rages, but the generally perceived wisdom is that The Eagle was the original gastropub.

It was the brainchild of Michael Belben and David Eyre. Both had wide experience of working in the London restaurant trade and both aspired to run their own venture, but London rents and start-up costs made this impossible. But the late 1980s and early 1990s were a time of great change in the pub industry as, following government legislation, many of the big breweries were forced to reduce the number of public houses under their direct control and this allowed the two men to pick up a cheap lease on The Eagle.

Food Revolution

Working to a tight budget, and with only a tiny kitchen space, they transformed the food on offer. So it was goodbye to pie, chips and beans and hello to a Mediterranean-style menu changing daily and boasting grilled meats and fish, pasta and salads, rustic bread and artisan olive oil. In time the kitchen moved to behind the bar, turning the art of cooking into something of a performance in its own right.

With its mismatched furniture (the original shabby chic?), acclaimed food (dubbed 'Pleb Med' by *Harper's* magazine), and lack of dining formality, the Eagle pretty much set the template for the gastropub as we know and (mostly) love it today. It was an instant success and a sensation on the London dining circuit. It helped, of course, that *The Guardian* newspaper was based only yards away and that Clerkenwell was already an area in a state of social flux.

There have been many imitators since, most of them very poor imitations at that, but The Eagle remains largely unchanged and was once described by Eyre himself as 'a stud farm for chefs'.

Records show that a tavern called the Golden Anchor stood on this site, formerly Coppice Row until being absorbed by Farringdon Road, from at least 1787. By the 1860s the pub was calling itself The Eagle. Many years later it is still flying high.

2

Finsbury and St Luke's

20. THE ARTILLERY ARMS, No. 102 Bunhill Row, EC1

These days The Artillery Arms, at the corner of Bunhill Row and Dufferin Street, is a well-appointed and welcoming public house located in the heart of Finsbury. But it wasn't always the case.

The Artillery Arms, Bunhill Row.

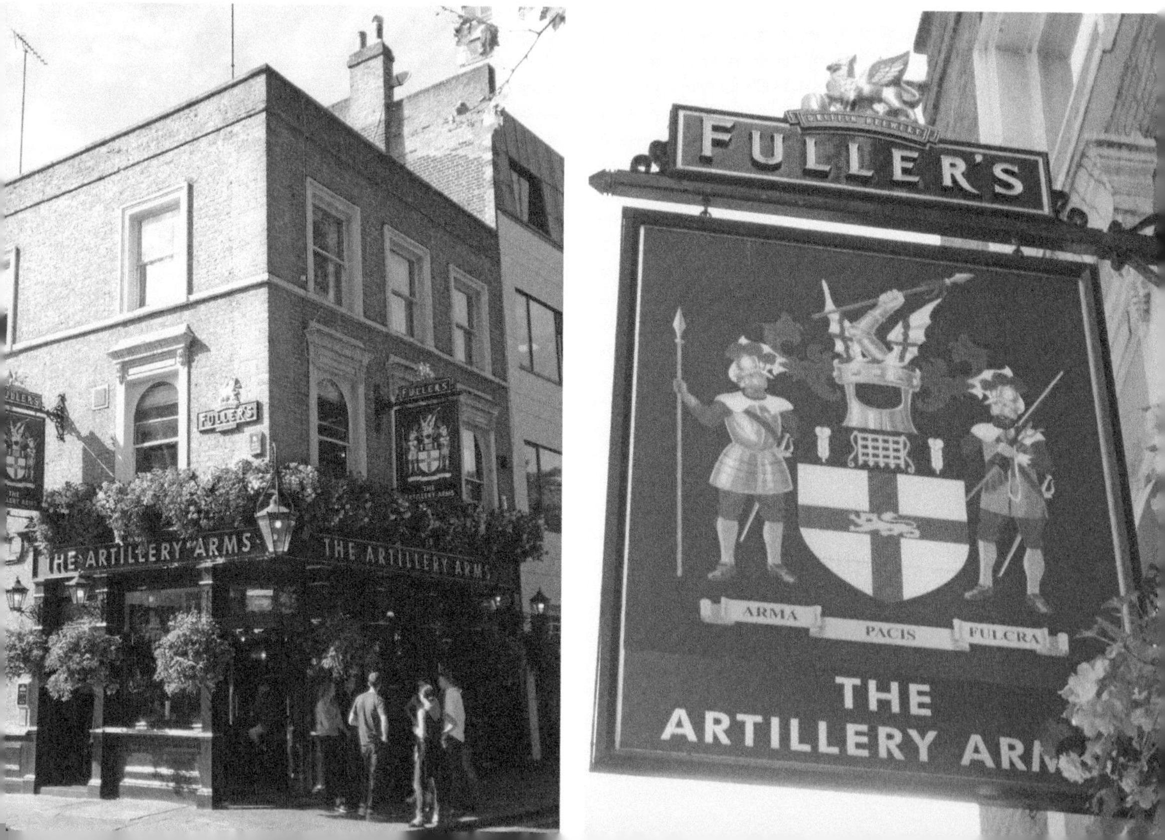

There has been a tavern on this site since at least 1830 and it originally traded as the Blue Anchor. Back then it was, according to several accounts of the time, a rough and ready place that enjoyed a degree of notoriety on account of the rat-baiting events held in a large area at the back of the pub.

Rat-baiting, a brutal so-called 'sport', involved placing a dog in an enclosed area alongside a number of live rats. It was then a question of how many rats the dog could kill and how long it would take him to do it.

The rats were usually caught in the fields surrounding the capital and the landlord of the time, Jimmy Shaw, would sometimes buy as many 700 a week. He had storage facilities at the pub to hold as many as 2,000 rodents at a time.

Tiny the Terrier

A particularly popular dog was a terrier by the name of Tiny, who appears to have been something of a superstar in the rat-baiting world. Twice, in 1847 and again in 1848, he managed to dispatch 200 unfortunate rats in less than an hour with 'time to spare' on both occasions.

The pub changed its name to The Artillery Arms in 1856 and the current building probably dates from a little later. The name was adopted on account of the Honourable Artillery Company (HAC), who are based just across the road. The HAC were granted their royal charter by Henry VIII in 1537 and are among the oldest military organisations in the world. They were originally based in Spitalfields, moving to their current location, the Artillery Ground, in 1658.

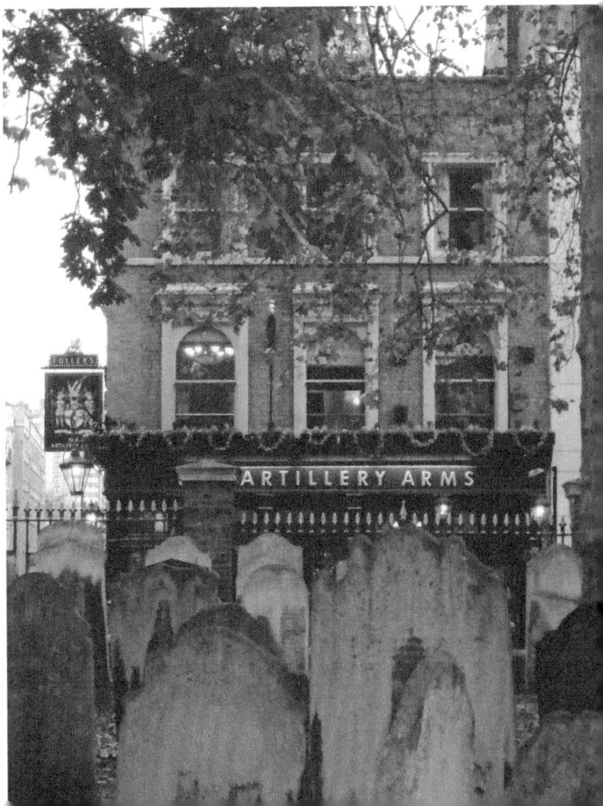

The Artillery Arms stands opposite Bunhill Fields cemetery.

The Artillery Ground has several claims to fame. Some of the earliest games of organised cricket were played here and on 15 September 1784, an Italian by the name of Vicenzo Lunardi took off on one of the earliest hot-air balloon flights to take place in England. A crowd of more than 200,000 turned out to watch, and Lunardi was accompanied on his flight by a dog, a cat and a pigeon in a cage. The pigeon must have been particularly confused.

The Artillery Arms, now a Fuller's pub, stands directly opposite Bunhill Fields, the famous Nonconformist cemetery. John Bunyan, Daniel Defoe and William Hogarth are all buried here.

21. OLD FOUNTAIN, No. 3 Baldwin Street, EC1

These days it's hard to imagine, as the traffic roars along City Road, but the neighbourhood of St Luke's was once largely rural and the Old Fountain pub, almost in the shadow of Moorfields Eye Hospital, is a link to that past.

There's been a tavern here since 1750, originally trading as the Old Fountain Knights. Today's pub, which also has another entrance in Peerless Street, looks to be of mid-Victorian stock with two once separate bars knocked through. It underwent some modernisation in the 1960s.

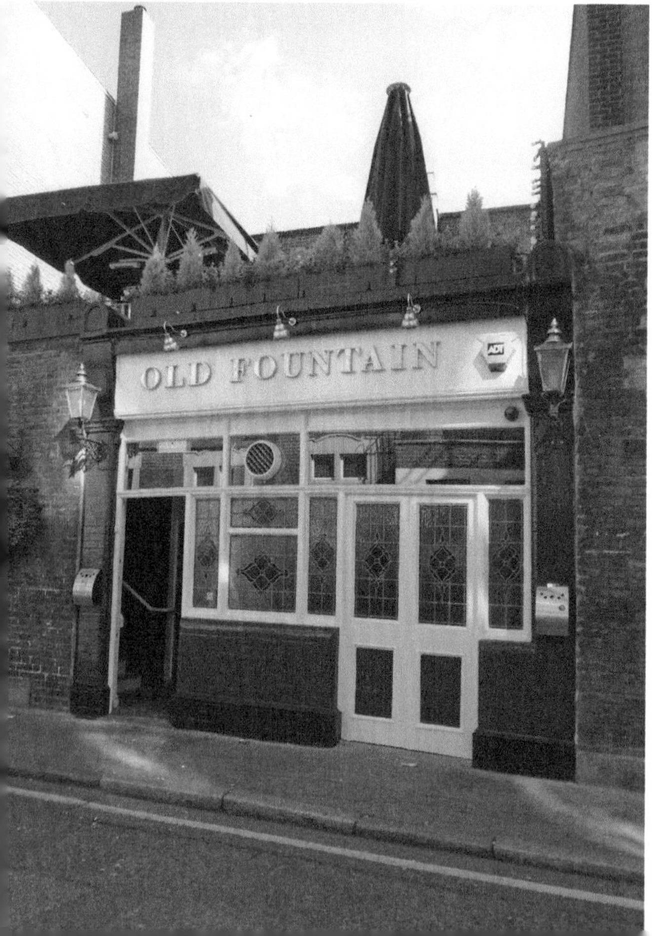

Old Fountain, Baldwin Street.

Its name is a reminder of a fascinating chapter in London history. Here, in 1743, a local jeweller named William Kemp purchased a large piece of land, roughly where today City Road and Old Street meet, upon which was situated an ancient pond, fed by a natural spring. The pond had been used for swimming by locals for many years and had claimed several lives. It was, thus, known as the Perilous Pond. This 'pond' must have covered a substantial area for it was also used for fishing.

The enterprising Kemp had grand plans for his new purchase and set about developing the pond and its surroundings as a visitor attraction. He installed marble steps descending into the water and laid a gravel bottom. A row of trees were planted to provide a natural screen.

Peerless Pool

Kemp's master stroke, however, was to ditch the Perilous Pond name and remarket it as Peerless Pool. The pool itself was 170 feet long, 108 feet wide and 5 feet deep. It is recognised as the first outdoor public swimming pool in London and proved hugely successful. A separate pond was reserved for fishing.

In 1805 Kemp sold out to a man called Joseph Watts and he set about draining the fishing pond and building upon it. Today's Baldwin Street, and the Old Fountain, sit upon part of that area of land.

Peerless Pool closed in 1850. In the years since it first opened the surrounding area had become built up and the idea of alfresco swimming against a backdrop of bricks and mortar was not so appealing. The land was promptly built upon.

The Old Fountain is still very much with us, however, and has been run by the Durrant family for the last fifty years or so. It was for many years a Whitbread house and a treasure trove of surviving, if defunct, brewery livery includes a mirror advertising 'Splendid Whitbread's Stout'. These days it is a great example of how an established old school pub has adapted and to some degree reinvented itself to embrace the craft and cask ale revolution.

22. THE BRITANNIA, No. 94 Ironmonger Row, EC1

The Britannia is that rare thing in twenty-first-century central London: a working-class street corner local that hasn't been converted into a gastropub or craft beer bar. Long may it stay that way.

The pub we have today was built in 1939, although there has been a tavern on the same site since 1842. The old parish of St Luke's is historically rich and traditionally working class, although the demographic is changing as the hipsters of Clerkenwell to the north and Hoxton to the east continue their pincer movement on the area.

Although only yards from Old Street's Silicon Roundabout, a fashionable quarter of London popular with technology and internet companies, the 'Brit's' clientele is mainly drawn from the surrounding council estates. Indeed there are some fine examples of progressive post-war council housing in the surrounding streets, courtesy of the old London Borough of Finsbury.

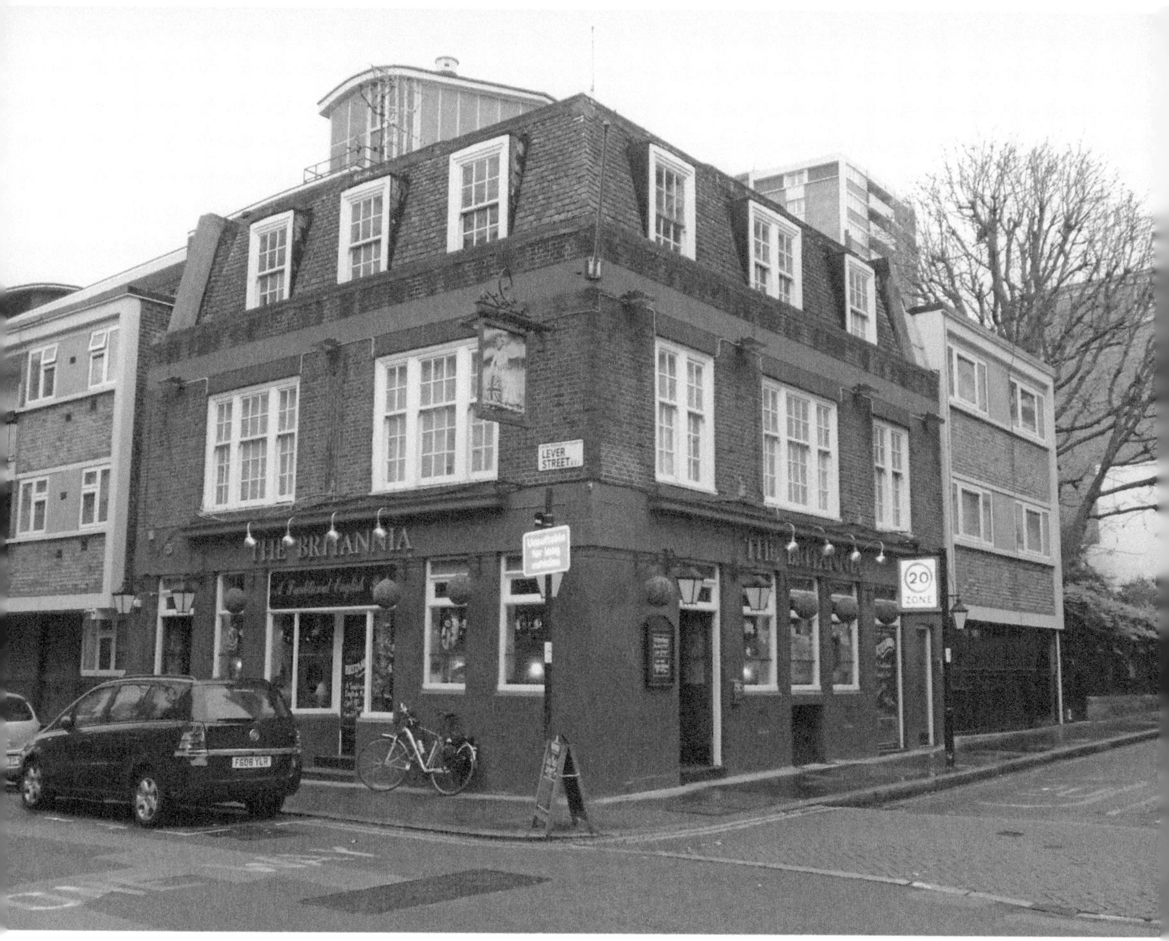

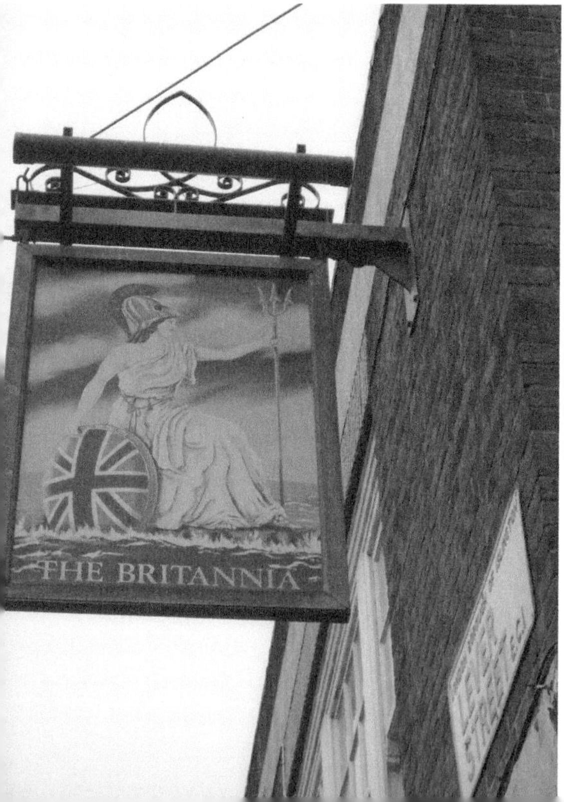

The Britannia, Ironmonger Row, St Luke's.

Brewing Giant

For most of its history the Britannia was controlled by the mighty Whitbread, one of the most famous names in British brewing. Samuel Whitbread, in partnership with brothers George and Thomas Shewell of the Goat Brewery on the corner of Old Street and Whitecross Street, established a brewery at Chiswell Street in 1750. It is widely regarded as the world's very first large-scale, mass-production brewery and, specialising in porter, was the biggest in Britain just eight years after starting up.

Whitbread were among the famous – for many people infamous – 'big six' that dominated British brewing for many years. However the company sold off all its brewing and beer interests in 2001 and are best known now for the Premier Inn and Costa Coffee chains.

The Chiswell Street brewery still stands today and you can stroll to it from the Britannia in ten minutes or so if you get your skates on. Alas, brewing ceased there in 1976, although Whitbread's famous horse-drawn drays continued to deliver locally into the early 1990s. There are some nice bits of brewery memorabilia to be seen in the pub today and they even sell Whitbread beer on keg – although these days it is brewed under the auspices of InBev, many, many miles from London, EC1.

23. THE SHAKESPEARE, No. 2 Goswell Road, EC1

When the sprawling and groundbreaking Golden Lane Estate was developed after the Second World War, almost every facet of life in the city was catered for. So, in addition to 1,400 flats and maisonettes, there was a swimming pool, a bowling green (now tennis courts), a nursery, a playground and also a community centre. There was also,

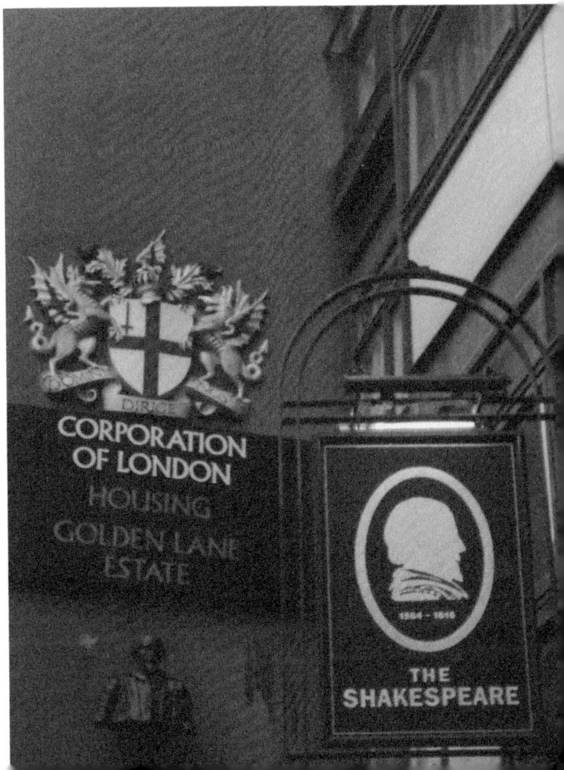

The Shakespeare, Aldersgate Street, part of the Golden Lane Estate.

located on the ground floor of the Crescent House block which faces Goswell Road, a row of shops and, to complete the jigsaw, The Shakespeare pub.

Development of the estate started in 1953 and wasn't completed until the mid-1960s. The Shakespeare opened its doors for the first time on 23 April, 1964, the anniversary of both the Bard's birth and death – or so we are led to believe.

Although we must consider it a 'modern' hostelry, it is worth bearing in mind that a few years ago it celebrated a half century of pouring pints. Ian Nairn, in his seminal *Nairn's London* of 1966, was, with some reservations, a fan of both the estate and the pub, describing the Shakespeare as 'modern, but without the decorative affectations that plague pub designers'.

Cripplegate

Although the estate is overseen by the Corporation of London, the 7.5-acre site was originally in the old borough of Finsbury and many residents of that borough were housed here – hence its inclusion here. A boundary change in 1994 means that the whole Golden Lane Estate now sits in the City of London, including the Shakespeare, although only just. The buildings directly opposite are in the London Borough of Islington, which swallowed up Finsbury in 1965.

This corner of the capital is, partly at least, historic Cripplegate, described by Tom Bolton in his wonderful 2014 book *Vanished City* as one of 'London's lost neighbourhoods'. The area was decimated by the Luftwaffe during the Blitz, hence the large-scale post-war rebuilding that saw, in addition to Golden Lane, the construction of the Barbican.

There has long been a pub presence at least roughly where today's Shakespeare stands, although changes over the years in street numbering rather cloud the issue. A pub called the White Hart was certainly recorded at No. 1 Goswell Road as early as 1850, later changing its name to the Corner Pin, which certainly ties in with today's location on the corner of Goswell Road and Fann Street.

However when the current pub was built, it was decided to name it after the nearby Shakespeare Tavern, which was demolished in the early 1960s. The Fortune Playhouse, where many of the Bard's works were performed, stood nearby and is remembered today by a plaque in the aptly named Fortune Street.

24. THE OLD IVY HOUSE, No. 166 Goswell Road, EC1

The once solidly working-class areas of Clerkenwell and St Luke's, effectively the old London Borough of Finsbury, which was swallowed up by Islington, have changed a lot in recent years, but Goswell Road remains something of an enigma and remains largely immune from the nearby gentrification. As, indeed, has the Old Ivy House, which, despite being spruced up somewhat by current owner Shepherd Neame, remains a solid and largely unremarkable boozer, indeed remarkably and reassuringly so.

The pub, a smallish mid-Victorian hostelry on the corner of Seward Street, claims to have occupied this site for 200 years and there are certainly records of it being here as early as 1837. It was for many years a Charrington house until, in the early 1980s, it took a leading role in what can only be described as a beer revolution.

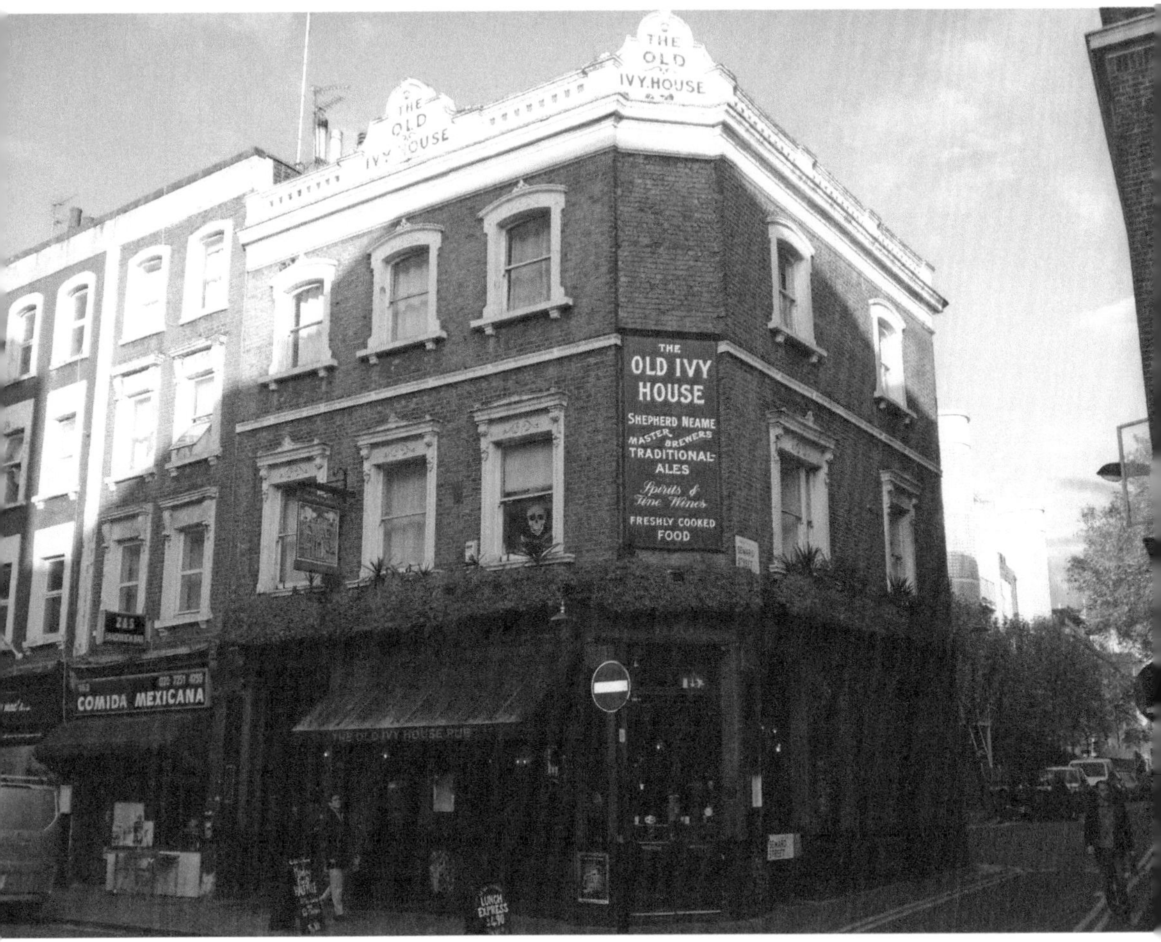

The Old Ivy House, Goswell Road.

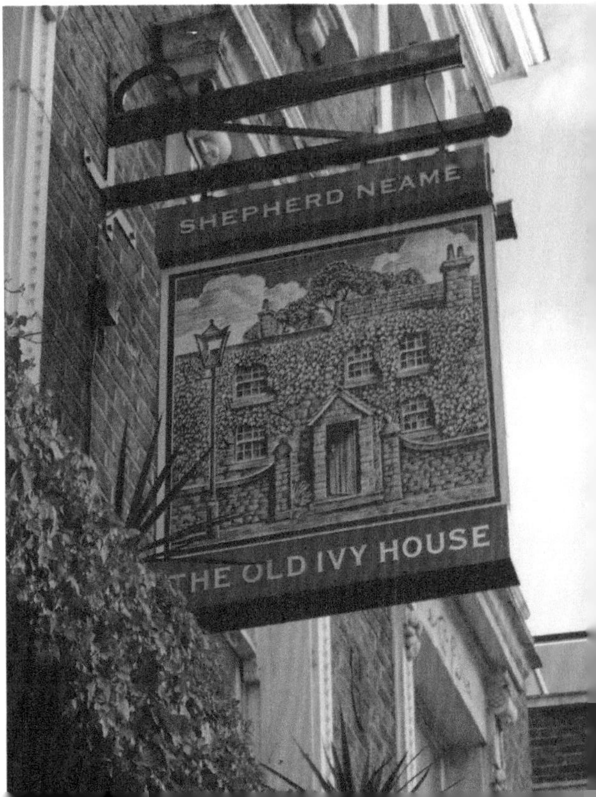

Bruce's Brewery

For much of the 1960s and 1970s the London drinking scene was a challenging one for the lover of real ale. The majority of pubs were controlled by the so-called 'big six', huge brewing and pub concerns that saw keg beer – pasteurised and artificially carbonated – as the way forward. As a result cask ale – that is beer which needed to undergo a secondary fermentation in the pub cellar and was served via hand-pulled gravity pump – was the exception rather than the norm.

In 1979 David Bruce, a brewing industry veteran looking for a new challenge, opened the Goose and Firkin brewpub in Borough Road, south London, where much of the ale on offer was made on the premises. It was also an artfully spit and sawdust affair that soon became hugely successful. So, in a short period of time, Bruce opened more pubs and in the early 1980s the Old Ivy House became the Pheasant and Firkin.

Here the cramped basement microbrewery could be observed via a glass floor and the pub, alongside several other Bruce establishments, soon became something of a real-ale Mecca. It was great fun while it lasted, but in 1988 Bruce sold-up and over the next decade or so the Firkin brand, and Firkin pubs, went through a number of different ownerships, including a period in the hands of Allied Domecq, the cask ethos diluted with every passing year. In 2001 Punch Taverns mercifully retired what was by then a rather tawdry and tarnished brand.

And so, in time, the Old Ivy House returned to its original name and the distinctly scruffy feel of the Firkin days disappeared. It remains, however, a dependable, no thrills local. I'll drink to that.

25. THE PEASANT, No. 240 St John Street, EC1

For the last decade of the nineteenth century the capital was gripped by an unprecedented pub-building boom that saw both wealthy pub proprietors and many of London's giant breweries invest heavily in ornate and often substantial hostelries. No expense was spared on lavish fixtures and fittings as some of the top architects and designers of the day set about transforming the pub landscape of the mighty metropolis.

The Peasant, or George and Dragon to give it its original name, is an early product of that boom. Standing proudly on the corner of St John Street and Percival Street, it is an imposing building, described somewhat dismissively, and to my mind unfairly, by Marc Girouard in his seminal 1984 book *Victorian Pubs* as 'big commercial Queen Anne'. It was built between 1889 and 1890, so right at the start of the boom, replacing a pub of the same name. Records show that the George and Dragon, in one form or another, had stood on this site as early as 1788.

The pub was built for William Pierpont, a noted London publican of the day, who had made a fortune in the pub trade and was prepared to invest further in the hope of big returns. He certainly aimed high with the George and Dragon. It was constructed by the noted building company of W. L. Kellaway to the designs of the even more noted architect Harry Isaac Newton, who specialised in public houses.

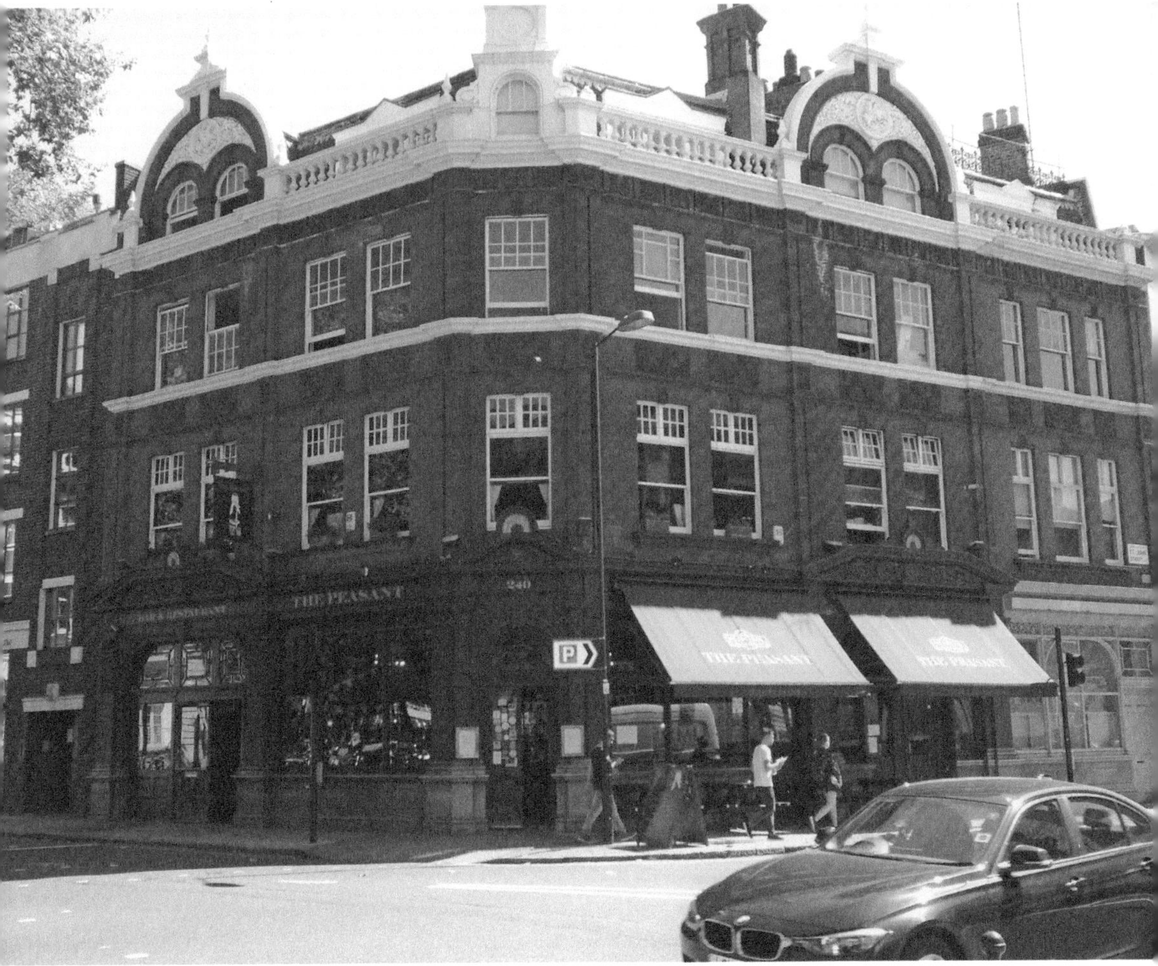

Above: The Peasant, St John Street.

Right: Tiled mural at The Peasant, St John Street.

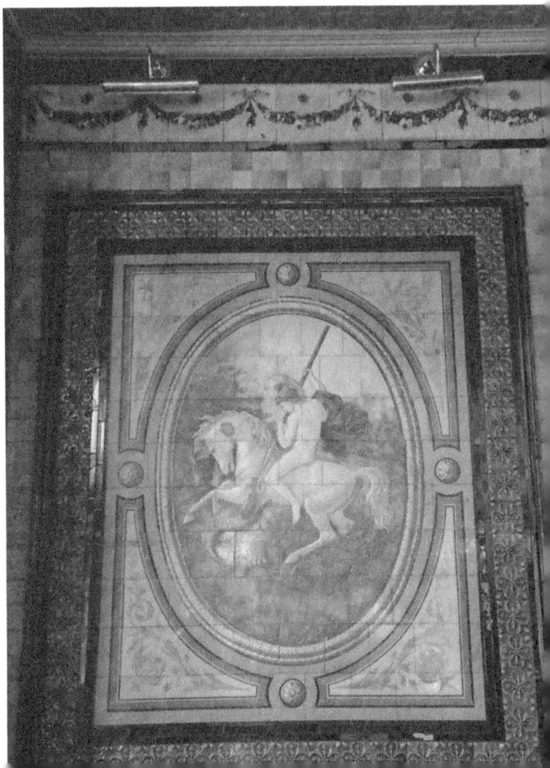

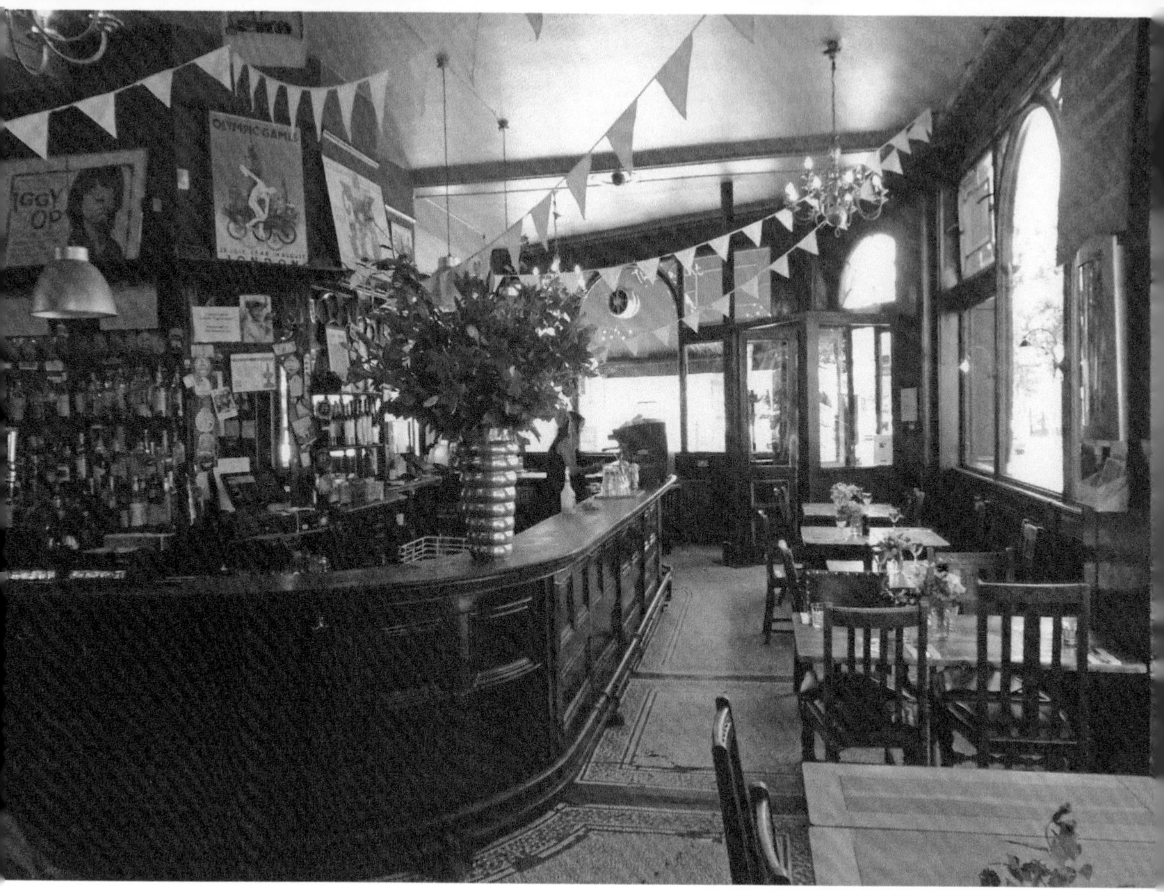

Main bar of The Peasant.

Tiled Mural

Newton made his name in the two decades immediately before the pub-building boom of the 1890s, and Girouard estimates he was responsible for ninety-six pubs between 1873 and 1891, which makes the George and Dragon a late addition to his canon.

Where there is boom there is usually bust, however, and that's exactly what happened in London. The returns on these grand and great pubs were, in most instances, not great enough to justify their existence and many a proprietor was declared bankrupt as a result.

Fortunately Newton's pub is still with us today. As is the grand horseshoe bar, much of the original mosaic floor and, the star of the show, a stunning tiled mural by Webb and Co. depicting George doing battle with the dragon. It's worth the admission price alone, so to speak.

The pub holds a very special place in my heart because this is where I had my very first pint with my dad, although it was a very different Clerkenwell back then. It has been the Peasant since the 1990s and these days much emphasis is placed on food and craft beer.

26. EXMOUTH ARMS, No. 23 Exmouth Market, EC1

The recent history of Exmouth Market, and of the Exmouth Arms, is the recent history in microcosm of many areas of central London. This is a story of change and of gentrification.

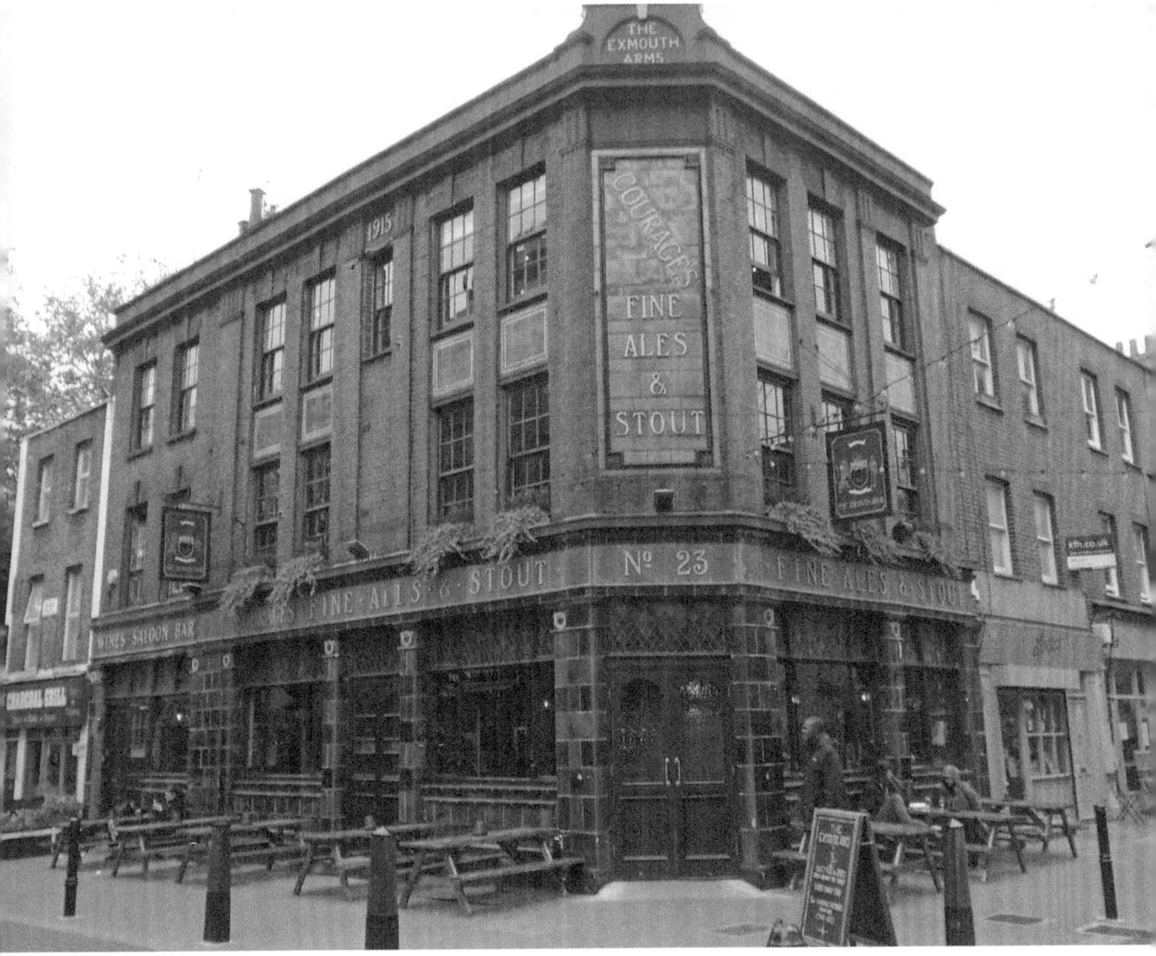

The Exmouth Arms, Exmouth Market.

Exmouth Street was so named in 1818 in honour of Admiral Pellew, a distinguished naval officer who became the first Viscount Exmouth, an honour bestowed upon him in 1816 after he led a fleet to victory at the Bombardment of Algiers, which in turn led to the release of more than a thousand Christian slaves.

There are records of beer being sold on this site as early as 1825 but the Exmouth Arms itself wasn't established until 1863. Today's rather fine building dates from a 1915 rebuild by the famous old Southwark brewer Courage. The company name can still be seen on the bold exterior, alongside some exquisite, if rather battered, green glazed tiles.

Street Market

A street market was sanctioned here in 1894 and Exmouth Street officially became Exmouth Market in 1939. The Exmouth Arms evolved into a classic old school London market public house that would once have been divided into two separate bars. Today, despite being knocked through, one door reads 'saloon bar' and another 'market bar'. As the street market trade declined, the pub became a popular destination for postal workers from the nearby Mount Pleasant Sorting Office.

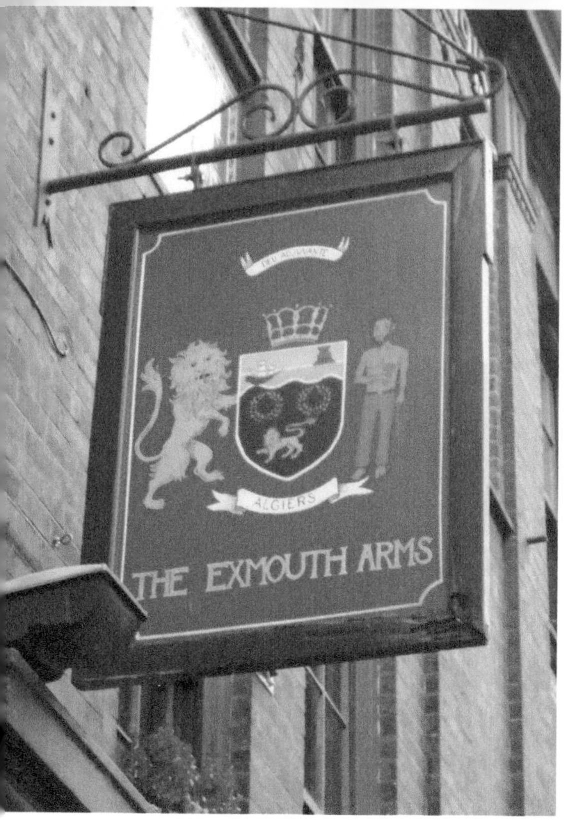

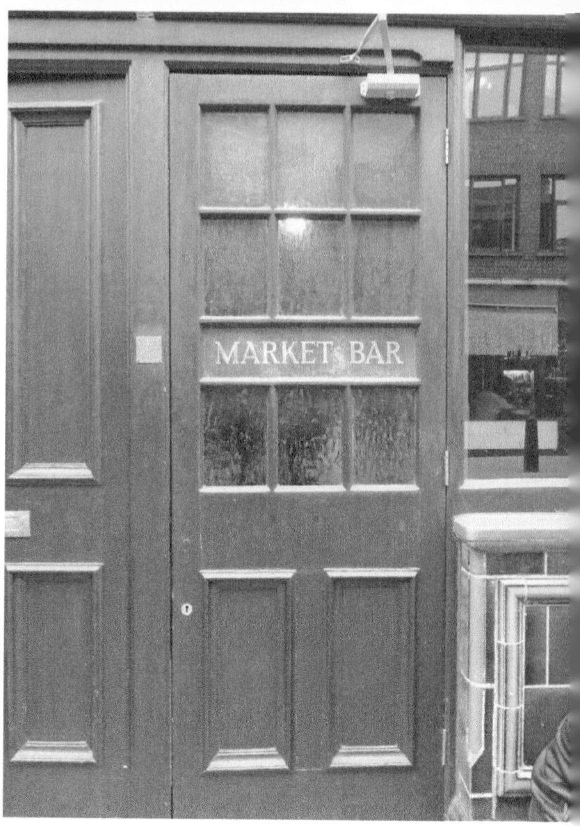

The Exmouth Arms was once a classic London street market pub.

Here then, in what might be termed north Clerkenwell, was a thriving traditional working-class street market, not as grand or substantial as many but a vibrant place nonetheless and absolutely essential to the lives of many local people. In 1968's *Geoffrey Fletcher's London*, the great chronicler of the post-war capital declared it 'one of the most attractive of the north London street markets'. It was, he wrote, a place where you could find 'cabbages and cauliflowers, bananas, brussels and budgie food', not to mention pie and mash.

In recent years the place has changed, almost beyond recognition for those of us who grew up nearby, and the fruit and veg stalls have gone as the hipsters have moved in. You'll struggle these days to find budgie food here, or even pie and mash, and your cauliflower is likely to be roasted and served with 'cashew nut dukkah, fried lemons, pickles and green tahini' in one of the street's numerous restaurants.

The Exmouth Arms, not surprisingly, is now a craft beer destination. It's an attractive enough place, with some original features retained, but is definitely not the scruffy street market boozer of yesteryear. Some people will tell you this is progress. I am not one of them.

27. THE BLACKSMITH AND THE TOFFEEMAKER, Nos 292–94 St John Street, EC1

If any student attending the City University – located opposite the Blacksmith and Toffeemaker – decided to perhaps write their thesis on the gentrification of central

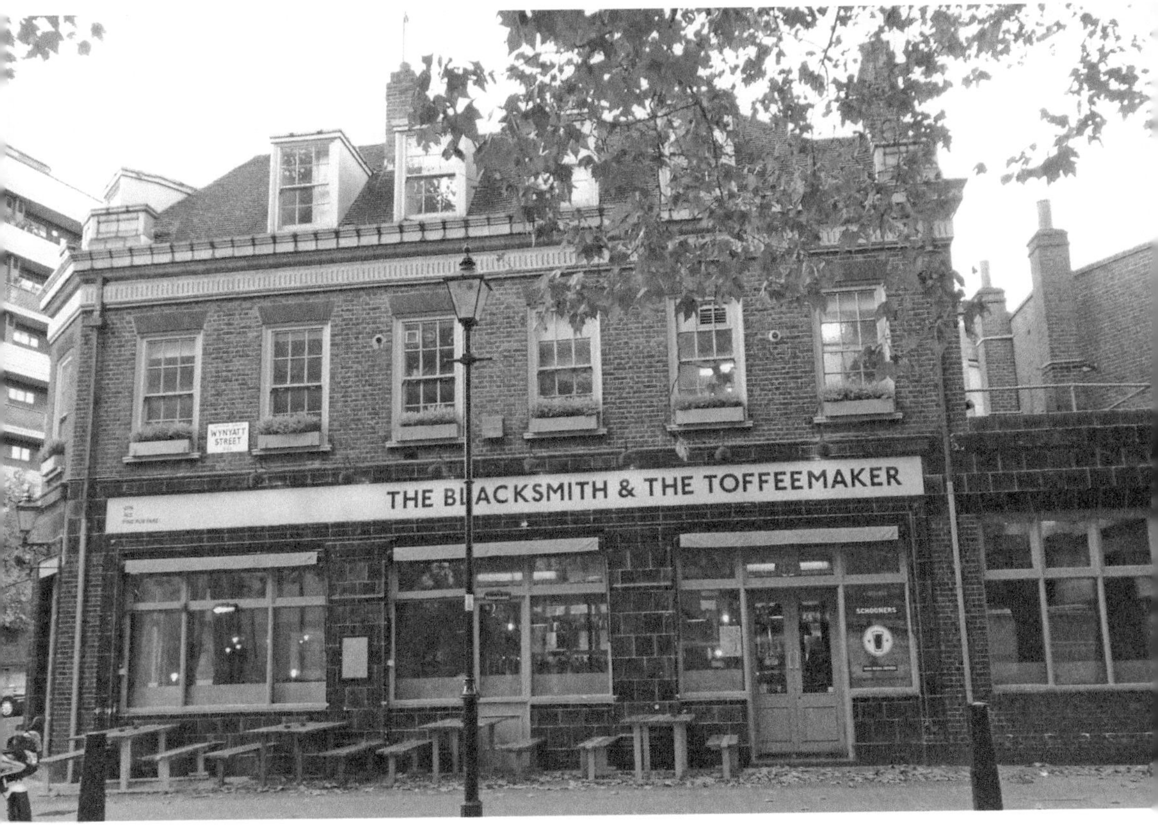

The Blacksmith and the Toffeemaker, St John Street.

London, they could do much worse than read up on the history of this particular hostelry, which in recent years has gone from being a sturdy corner street local into something of a student and hipster hangout.

The pub stands on the corner of St John Street and Wynyatt Street. For centuries St John Street would have been a busy and congested artery, one of the major routes into the City from the north used by drovers to transport livestock to Smithfield for slaughter. To cater for the vast numbers of salesmen, drovers and carriers involved in the meat trade many taverns were built, although they started to decrease after the livestock trade was moved north to Copenhagen Fields in 1855. Smithfield Market, more or less as we know it today, opened in 1868.

Before The Blacksmith and the Toffeemaker was The Blacksmith and the Toffeemaker, a name it had foisted upon it in 2012, it was from 2006 the Queen Boadicea. From the year 2000 until that point it was called the Bull. For generations of people, however, the pub will always be known as the New Red Lion, an unpretentious and lively working-class local frequented by a colourful roll call of characters. As such it is much missed.

Jake Thackery

Records of a pub on this site date back as far as 1809 and it was originally called simply the Red Lion. But with the much more famous Old Red Lion located a few hundred yards north along St John Street, the prefix 'New' was adopted at some point in the late nineteenth century, to avoid confusion one can only assume.

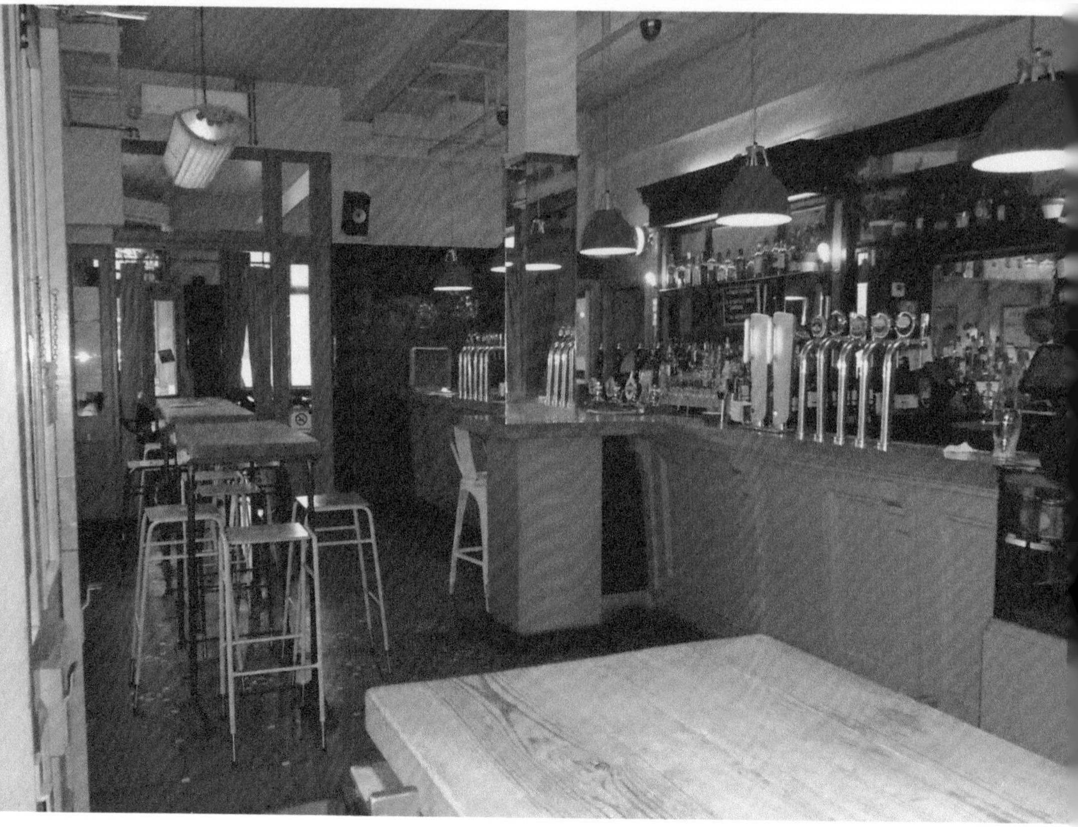

The Blacksmith and the Toffeemaker, St John Street.

The current building, which despite being rather messed about with internally in recent years, retains an air of restrained art deco combined with a distinctly utilitarian feel and dates from a 1923/24 rebuild. It was a Watney Combe Reid pub for many years and the bar back still proclaims 'Welcome to this Watney's House.' A rare surviving feature surrounded by much kitsch and artifice.

The pub was taken over in 2012 by Matt Rix and Marc Dalla-Riva. With little, if any regard for local history, it was renamed The Blacksmith and the Toffeemaker after a track by cult Yorkshire folk singer Jake Thackery. Rix, apparently, is a huge Thackery fan. So he's to blame. Rix, not Thackery that is.

28. HARLEQUIN, No. 27 Arlington Way, EC1

The Harlequin is one of those increasingly rare things: a London pub with an element of the well-kept secret about it. Tucked away in a sleepy Finsbury backstreet just behind Sadler's Wells Theatre, it is a small one-room boozer that caters to a mixture of locals and theatregoers. A bell still sounds in the bar to warn drinkers that the start of a performance next door is imminent. You can almost smell the greasepaint.

Arlington Way, previously Arlington Place and, until as recently as 1936, Arlington Street, was developed between 1822 and 1824 and the Harlequin was part of a row of seventeen terraced properties on the east side. There was an almost mirror terrace development standing opposite but this was the victim of Second World War bomb damage, as today's buildings confirm.

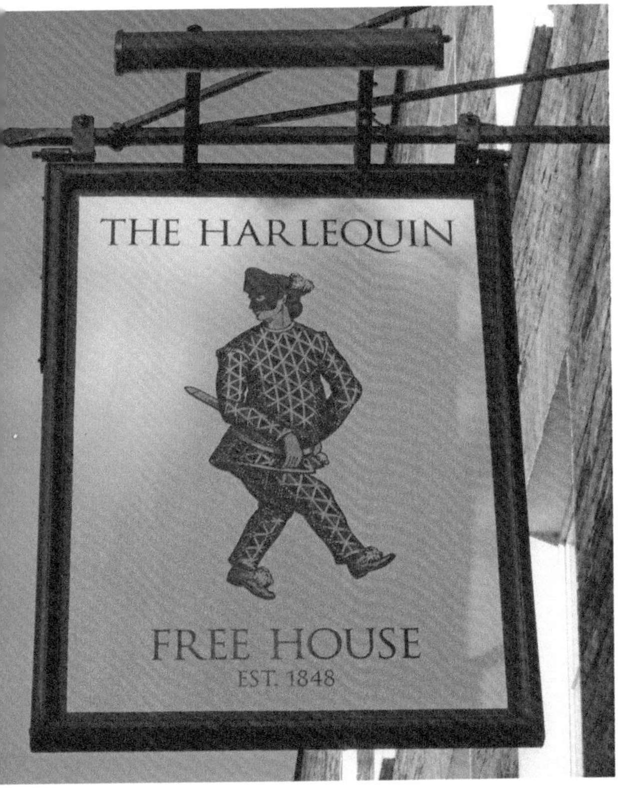

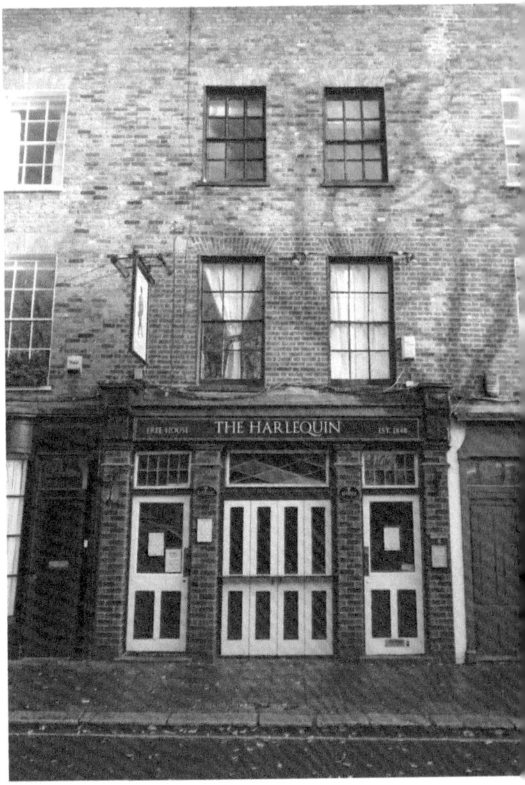

The Harlequin, Arlington Way.

The earliest mention of a public house here comes in 1848 when a 'beer shop' is recorded at No. 27, and it was certainly trading as The Harlequin by 1894, under the control of the famous east London brewer Mann Crossman and Paulin. They oversaw the transformation of the pub frontage from its original bowed shop front style, an example of which can still be seen next door at No. 26, into its existing form, complete with beautiful green glazed tiling.

Joseph Grimaldi

The pub's name was inspired by Joseph Grimaldi, who for many years was a giant of the London stage and had a strong association with Sadler's Wells. An actor, comedian and dancer capable of amazing athletic feats, he was widely reckoned to be the most popular English entertainer of his day. He made his first appearance at the Wells in 1781, 'in the character of a monkey' according to Walter Thornbury in *Old London.*

It was Grimaldi who, effectively, established *commedia dell'arte* in England, although he put his own distinct spin on the form, helping to cement the harlequinade as a genre in English theatre. A truly remarkable man, Grimaldi perhaps did more than anyone in defining the character of the modern clown and it is as a result of his influence that clowns are still referred to this day as Joeys.

A Londoner born and bred, Grimaldi lived at several addresses within stumbling distance of today's Harlequin, and like many a thespian before and since was fond of a tipple when the fancy took him. He never, alas, visited this particular hostelry for he died in 1837, more than a decade before the pub was established.

3

Around The Angel and Upper Street

29. OLD RED LION, No. 418 St John Street, EC1

The Old Red Lion claims to have been on its current site since 1415, which would make it the oldest surviving public house in London, so it comes as no surprise that the place is so rich in history.

With front and back entrances, the Old Red Lion is also known as 'the in and out'.

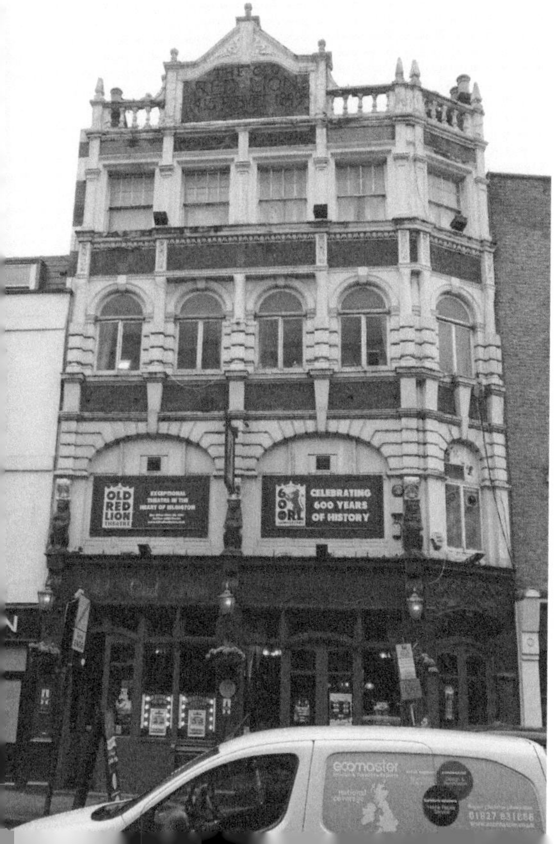

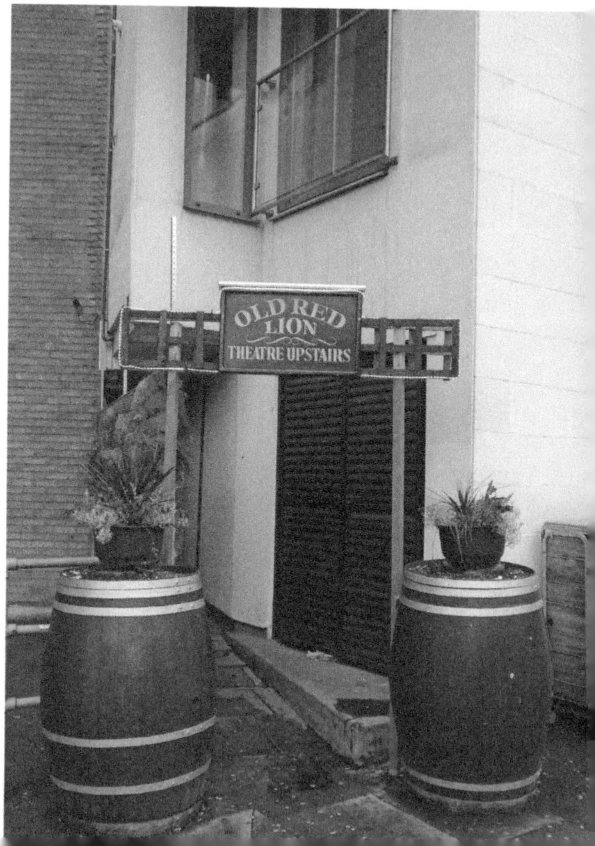

At around 600 years old, its antiquity has been noted by generations of Londoners down the ages. When the pub was sold at auction in 1871, it was billed with some fanfare by the auctioneers as 'one of the oldest established houses in the Metropolis'.

St John Street was the main route to the City and Smithfield from the north, so was busy with drovers and their livestock on the way to market. Originally the Redde Lyon, the pub was popular with this travelling clientele. It briefly changed its name to the Welsh Harp during the 1730s but was soon trading once more as The Red Lion. It appears to have adopted the 'Old' prefix around 1840.

The pub has been rebuilt many times and the current structure dates from 1899, with entrances in both St John Street and Goswell Road. This earned it the nickname of the 'in and out' with the London black cab fraternity on account of some passengers who would enter via one door 'to pick up a friend' and exit via another without paying their fare. It was designed by Eadle and Myers with the build undertaken by Charles Dearing and Sons. It has enjoyed Grade II listing since 1994 and retains some surviving internal cut-glass screens from when it was divided into a number of separate bar areas.

Thomas Paine

A claim was made in 1815 by the Revd Joseph Nightingale that in the Red Lion around 1790 'was written that curious engine of political mischief *The Rights of Man* by the notorious Thomas Paine'. However, a similar claim is made for the old Angel Inn that once stood only yards away. It is entirely possible, indeed likely even, that Paine spent time in both establishments.

In 1974 Pauline and Tony Sheriff-Geary took over and in 1979, in a small first-floor space, the Old Red Lion Theatre staged its first production. It continues to thrive. The Sheriff-Geary's remained until the year 2000 and their tenure marked a golden age for the pub, its customers a mix of thirsty locals and familiar faces from the worlds of television, film and stage.

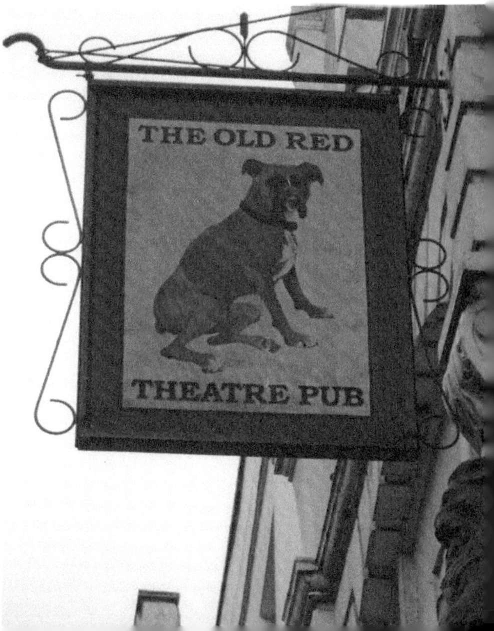

The Old Red Lion, St John Street.

Today it remains one of London's most characterful pubs, although the replacement hanging sign depicting a boxer dog seems like an odd way to celebrate 600 years of history. It's a cute dog, make no mistake, but no match for a roaring red lion.

30. THE CHARLES LAMB, No. 16 Elia Street, N1

The Charles Lamb is a rare example of a surviving, and by the look of it thriving, backstreet local that hasn't been closed and converted into residential use. Long may that continue.

The pub, compact and well-positioned, was built in 1839. That same year Queen Victoria proposed to Prince Albert, which would explain the pub's original name – the Prince Albert.

It remained the Prince Albert for almost 160 years but in 2005 was renamed the Charles Lamb. As you might gather from elsewhere in this book, the renaming of old pubs is a bit of a bugbear of mine and in an ideal world the Prince Albert would still be the Prince Albert. However, there is a locally historic justification for the adoption of the current name, which can't be said, for instance, of the nearby Blacksmith and Toffeemaker.

Charles Lamb was a writer best known for his poetry and essays. In the year 2000 his poem *The Old Familiar Faces* was voted one of the most 'popular poems of childhood' in a poll carried out by *Radio Times* magazine.

The Charles Lamb, Elia Street.

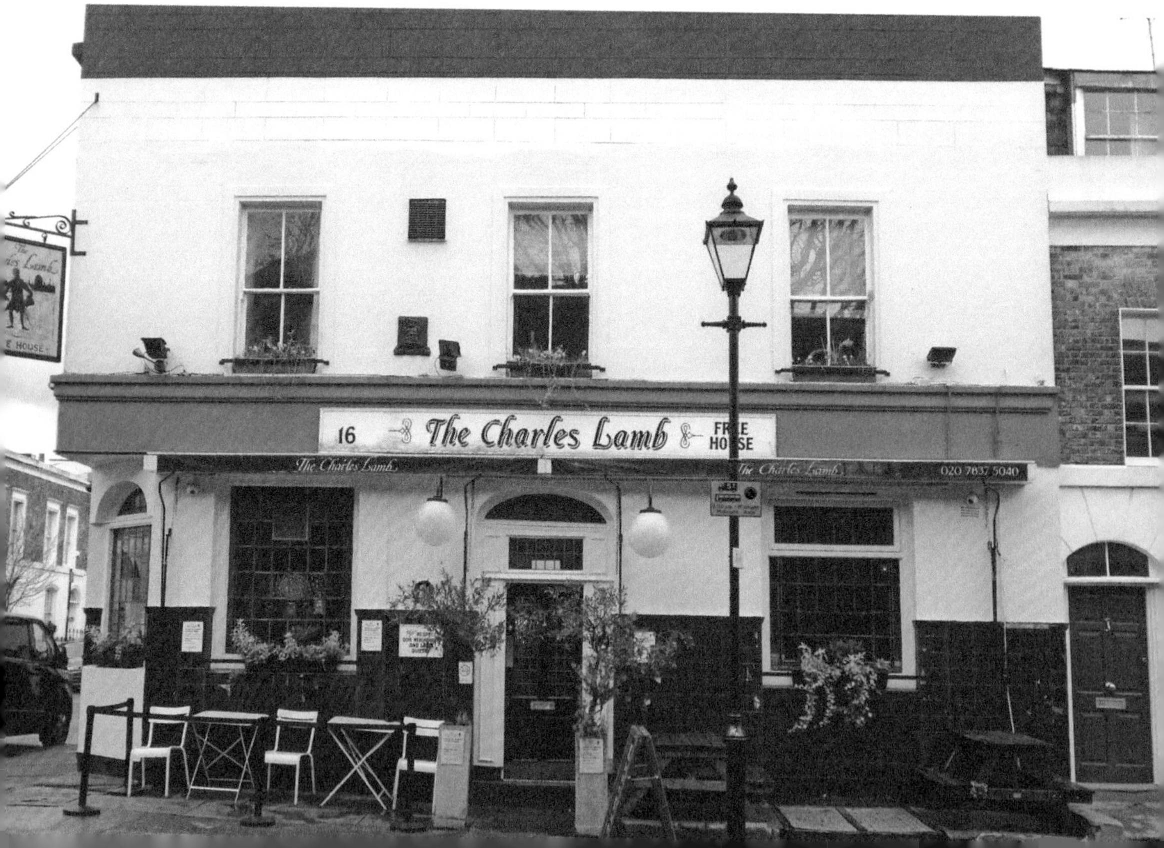

Elia Street

One of Lamb's many biographers, EV Lucas, described him as 'the most lovable figure in English literature'. Between 1823 and 1827 he lived with his sister in Colebrooke Cottage, a small dwelling 'rough with old books' that stands just yards from today's pub and is marked by an old brown London County Council plaque.

Lamb's best-known works are his *Tales From Shakespeare*, a book designed to make the Bard's works child-friendly, and the collection *Essays of Elia*. Elia was Lamb's pen name while writing for *The London Magazine* and would shortly after Lamb's death in 1834 inspire the name Elia Street.

The pub was originally built for the east London brewer Charrington, who operated from the famous old Anchor Brewery in Mile End. For many years their familiar Toby Jug logo adorned the pub's exterior. It seems, alas, to have disappeared, but thankfully some beautiful brown glazed tiles have survived.

Today the pub is a freehouse, although whether Lamb himself would have approved or not is uncertain. The writer struggled to control his drinking for much of his adult life and in 1813 wrote an essay titled *Confessions of a Drunkard*. Perhaps the temptation of having a pub on his doorstep might have proved too much.

31. THE THREE JOHNS, No. 73 White Lion Street, N1

The Three Johns is among a number of once fairly unremarkable working-class pubs in and around Chapel Market that in recent years have been stylishly transformed into achingly hip craft beer destinations.

The Three Johns, White Lion Street.

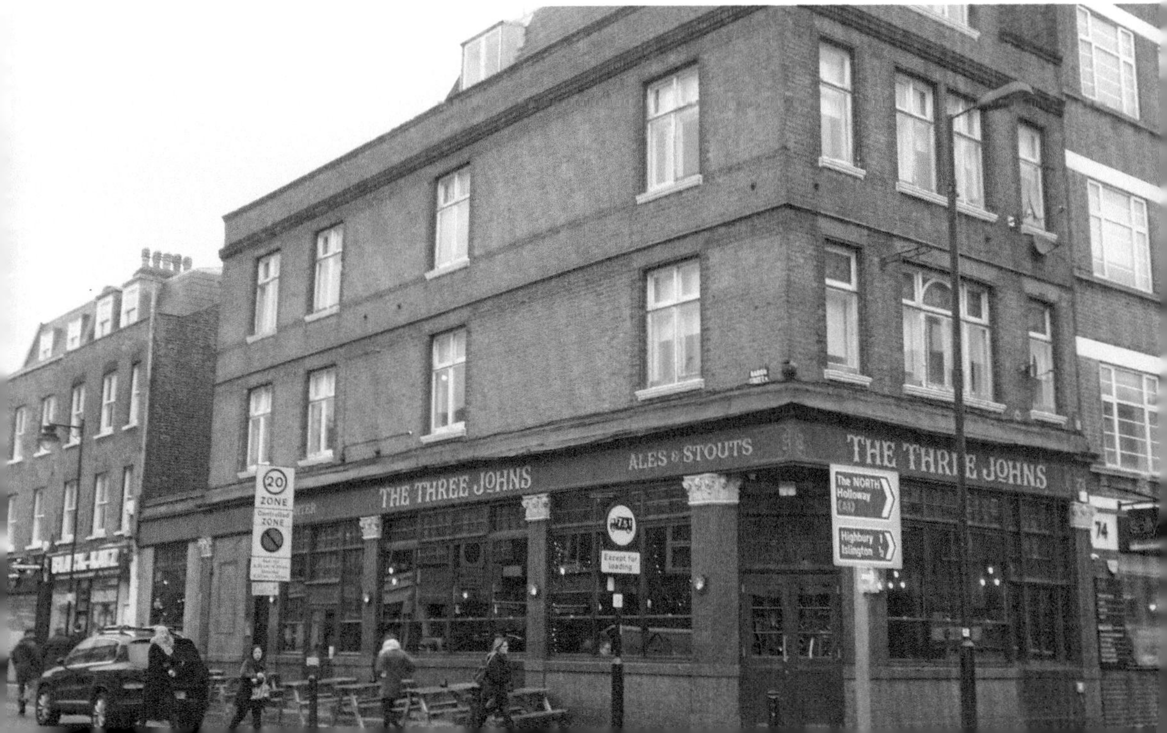

A big, handsome old pub standing on the corner of Baron Street and White Lion Street, records show that a hostelry of one sort or another has stood here since the 1780s. White Lion Street itself was developed from the 1770s onwards and is named after the famous old Whyte Lion Inn, which can be traced back to the late sixteenth century. It was rebuilt rather lavishly in 1898, although long ago closed as a public house. The building is still with us today, at No. 25 Islington High Street, and now houses a bank.

The current Three Johns dates from a rebuild courtesy of Watney Combe Reid carried out between 1899 and 1901. The name was changed briefly to the Hobgoblin around 2008 and then to the Fallen Angel. It was then, thankfully only briefly, the Jay Cubed before reverting to its original name around 2014.

Radical Figures

Perhaps the most interesting thing about the pub is the derivation of its original name, and for many years a plaque outside explained who exactly the three Johns in question were.

John Wilkes, the best known of the trio, was a leading radical figure for much of the eighteenth century, who made a name for himself as both a journalist and as a high-profile politician who spent time as both an alderman and a Member of Parliament. He also spent time in the Tower after a spat with George III.

Wilkes turned decidedly less radical in old age. In 1774 he became Lord Mayor of London and in 1780 was declared a 'hero' for his actions during the Gordon Riots when he led the defence of the Bank of England, quite likely coming up against men who had once openly supported him. The other two Johns were John Horne, a supporter of Wilkes, and John Glynn, his lawyer.

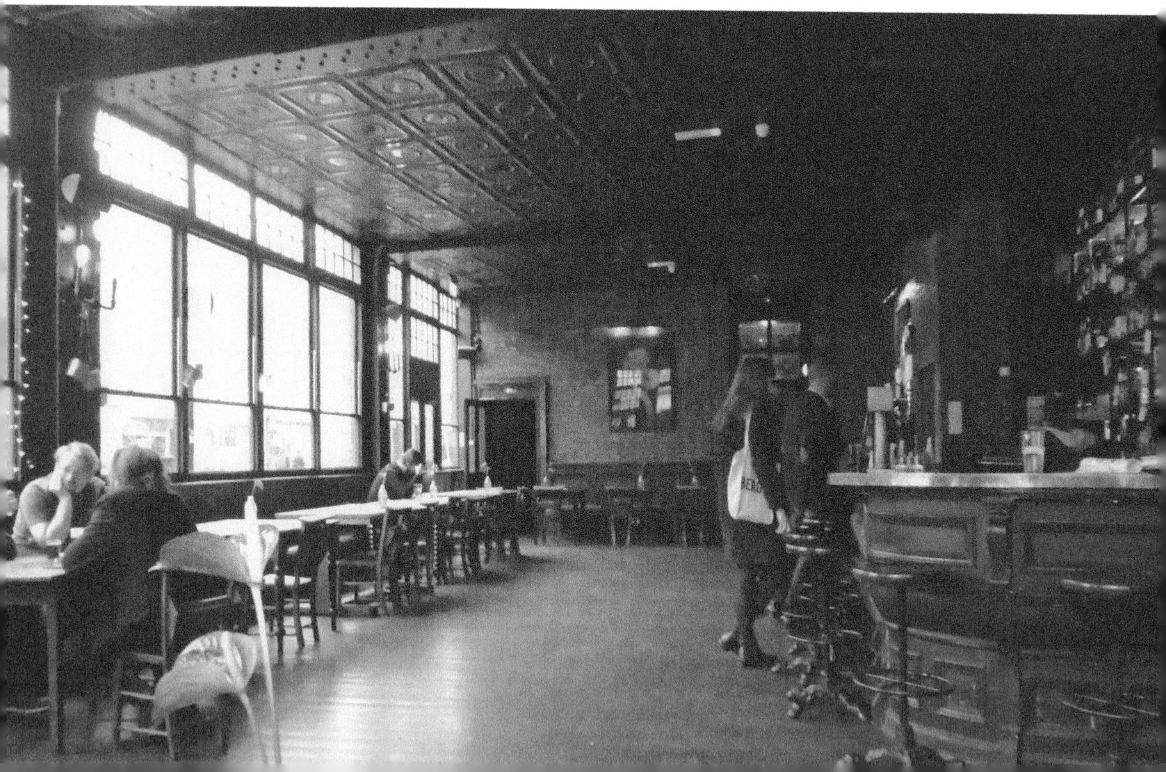

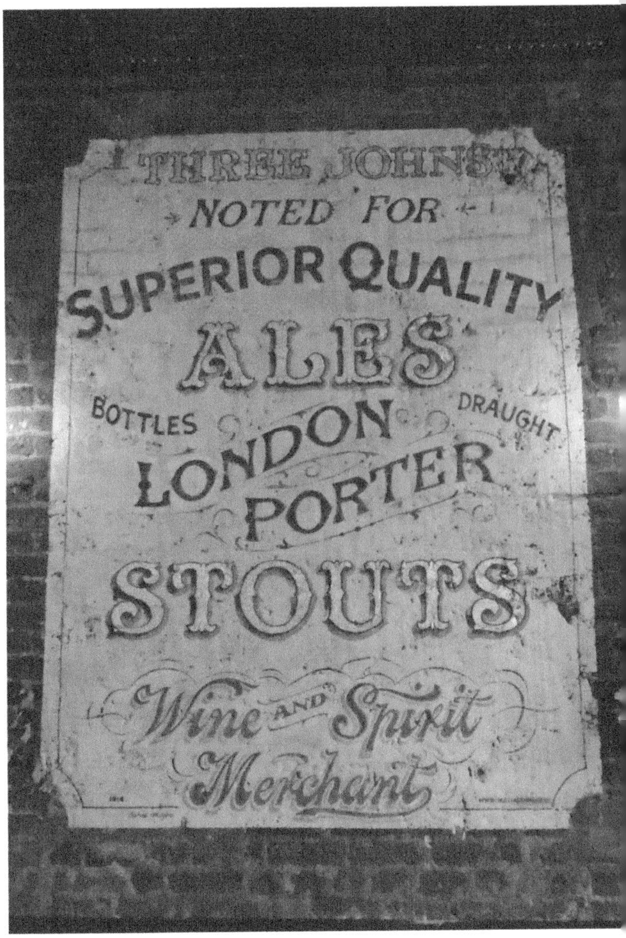

Opposite and right: Inside The Three Johns, White Lion Street.

All of which confirms that this part of London has long been a hotbed of political radicalism, a state of affairs that continues to this day: a certain Jeremy Corbyn has been Member of Parliament for the adjoining constituency of Islington North since 1983.

32. ISLAND QUEEN, No. 87 Noel Road, N1

There were once many pubs breaking up the leafy terraces of Islington, but over the years the majority have either been converted into residential use or turned into restaurants. So raise a glass to the Island Queen, still offering beer and cheer to the great and the good of north London 160-odd years on and counting.

The Island Queen first opened its doors in 1851, although this particular stretch of Noel Road was called Hanover Street back then. Hanover Yard still runs down one side of the pub. It enjoys Grade II listing and, although there have been some less than sympathetic changes in the post-war years, its interior is spectacular in places.

This is the result of a makeover in 1889, and another in 1897, and although the scale is small compared to some other London pubs, some exquisite etched glass and 'colonial'-style painted mirrors give the place the air of a gin palace. The island bar-back, meanwhile, is a thing of some beauty. The pub, not surprisingly, is listed in CAMRA's *Regional Inventory for London* for having an interior of 'specific historic interest'.

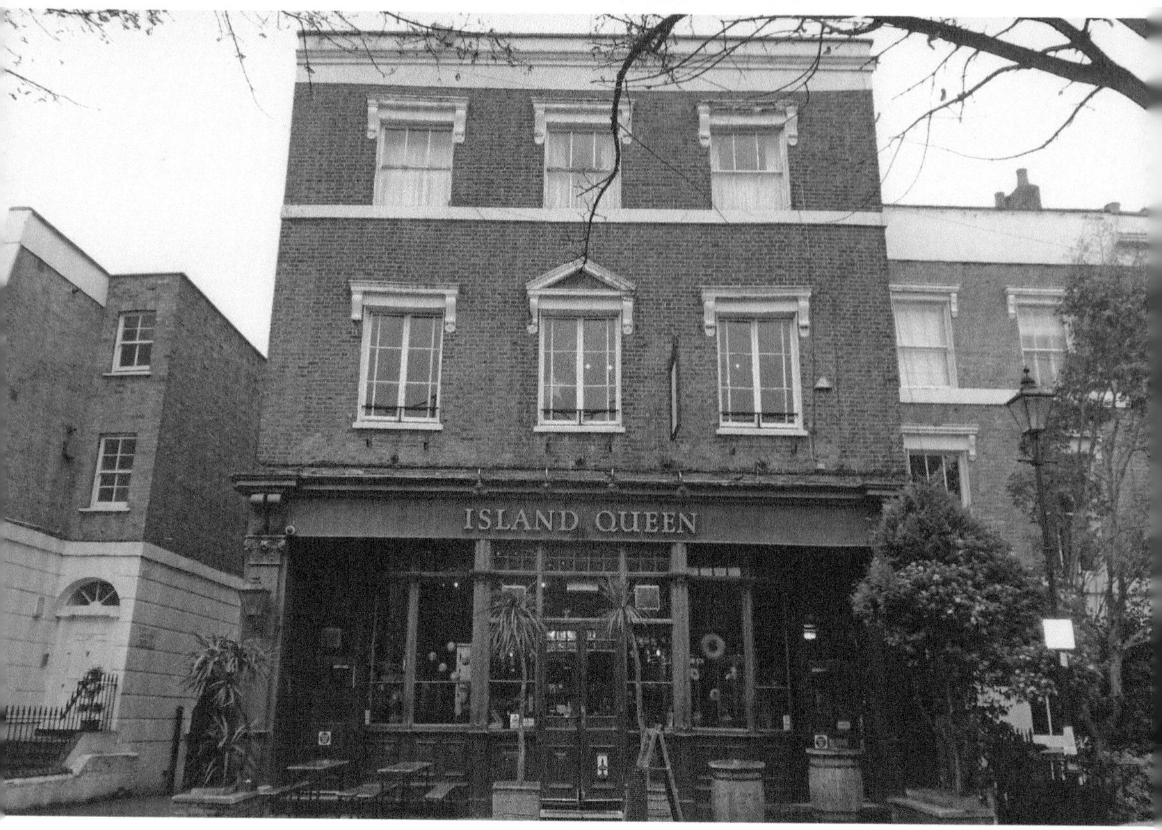

The Island Queen, Noel Road.

Joe Orton

For most of the 1960s, if you had popped into the Island Queen for a quick one, there was a good chance you might have found the playwright Joe Orton and his lover Kenneth Halliwell holding court while knocking back the brown and mild.

The two men lived together in a tiny top-floor bedsit just yards from the Island Queen, although as has been well documented their relationship was a volatile one. The two were living here when, in May 1962, they were convicted of 'larceny, malicious damage and wilful damage' of a number of books from Islington library in Essex Road. They were each sentenced to six months in prison.

Orton, of course, would later find fame as the writer of such bitingly satirical and subversive plays as *Entertaining Mr Sloane* and *Loot,* but on the night of 9 August 1967, he was bludgeoned to death by Halliwell, who then took his own life with an overdose of Nembutal.

Despite the craft beer and gastropub grub on offer today, Orton's ghost would certainly recognise the twenty-first century Island Queen as the pub he frequented many years ago.

33. THE CROWN, No. 116 Cloudesley Road, N1

The conservation area of Barnsbury is one of London's great unspoilt neighbourhoods, a leafy enclave of Islington that despite its close proximity to several very busy roads manages to retain a distinct village feel about it. Perhaps that's why The Crown, the

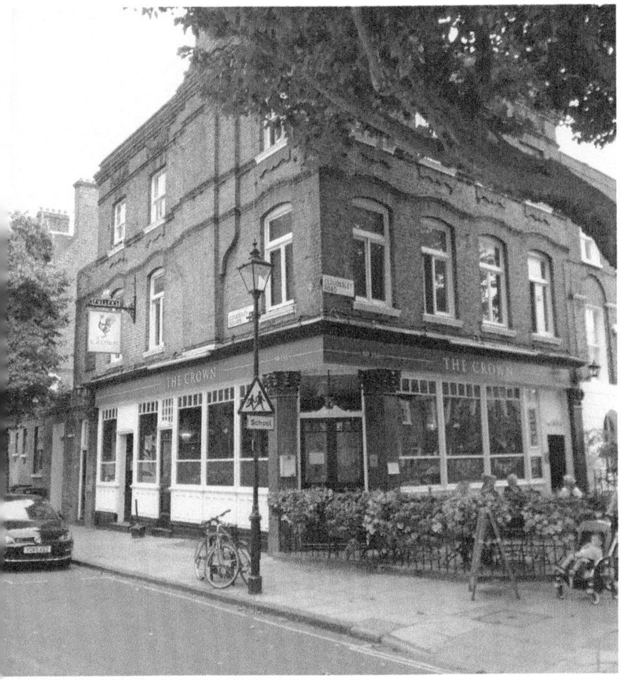

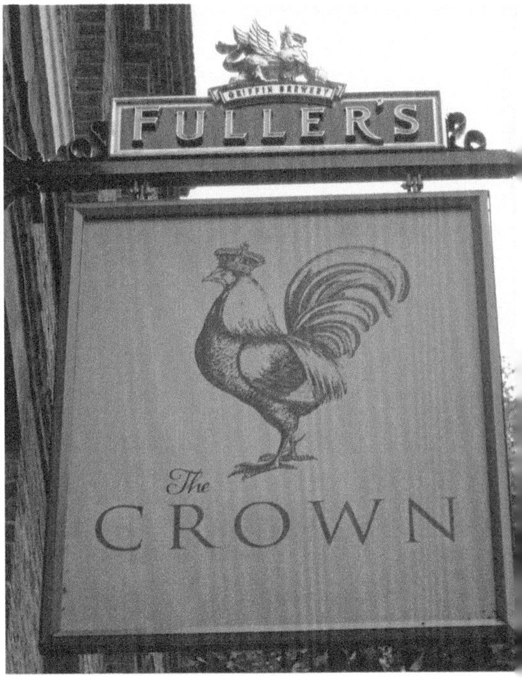

The Crown, Cloudesley Road.

area's best-known pub, remains such a fine, handsome and ever-so-slightly superior establishment, open to all, as long as you remember to wipe your feet first.

Plans for the development of the Cloudesley Estate, named after Tudor mover and shaker Richard Cloudesley, who once owned much land locally, were first mooted in 1812. Cloudesley Place came first with Cloudesley Square laid out in 1825, dominated by Sir James Barry's Holy Trinity Church, which owes more than a passing nod to King's College, Cambridge, and does rather overshadow all around it.

Cloudesley Road followed a little later and there are records of a hostelry, probably where today's Crown is sited, certainly as early as 1837. The current building dates from the late nineteenth century. It's a modest but elegant affair and one of north London's finest surviving examples of a largely intact late Victorian public house. It was Grade II listed in 1994.

Snob Screens

The pub interior is these days largely opened up, but would once have been divided into a number of separate bars. It is not beyond the bounds of possibility that back in the day the well-to-do occupants of some of the surrounding grand houses would have sipped their pale ale in the saloon bar, while at the same time members of their domestic staff were quaffing porter in the public bar next door.

That would certainly explain the surviving snob screens on the counter, which are possibly original but almost certainly not in their original position. A snob screen was a small pane of etched glass mounted on a pivoted fitting, the idea being that the middle-class drinker could see his social inferior but not vice versa. It also meant that eye contact with the person serving you could be avoided. The Crown, I am delighted to report, is an altogether more egalitarian place these days.

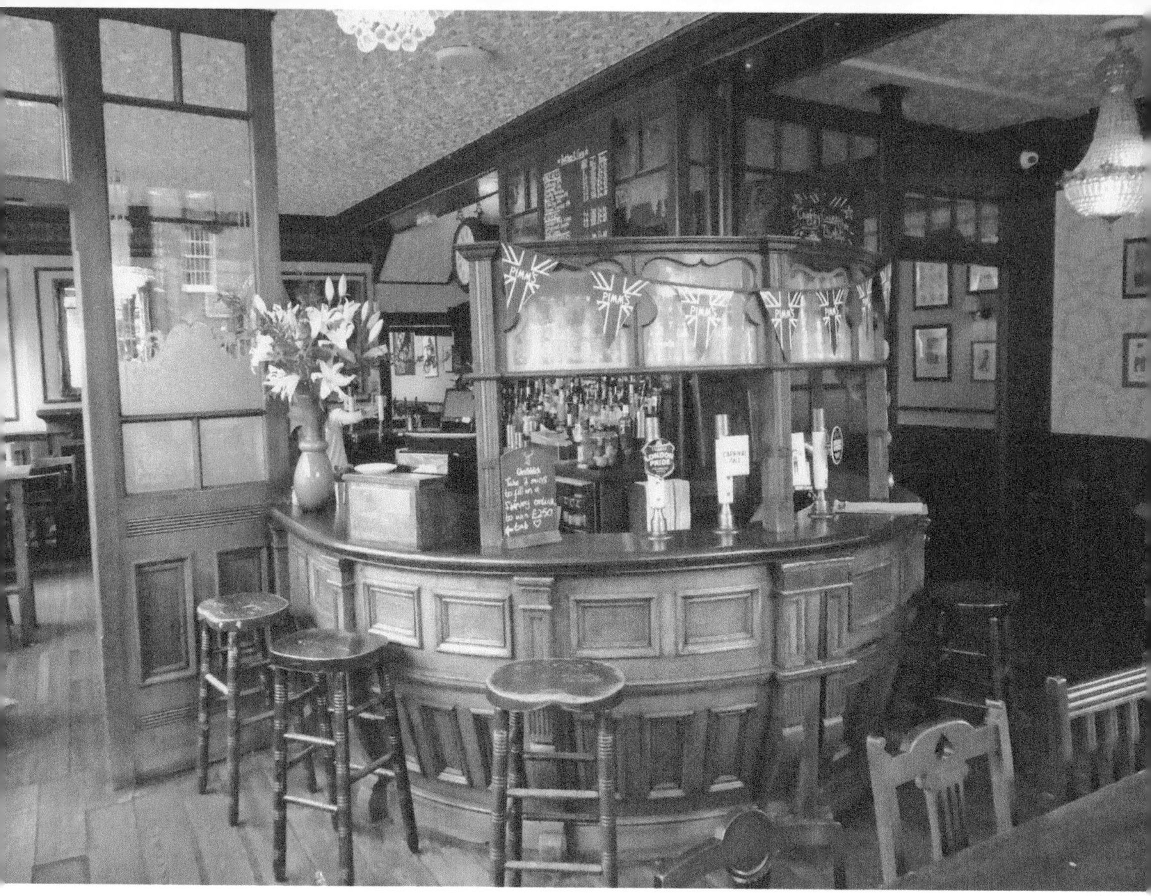

The Crown, Barnsbury, is Grade II listed.

The pub also features many fine examples of original etched and cut glass. It features in CAMRA's 2004's *Regional Inventory for London* and its rich design heritage looks to be safe in the hands of current owner Chiswick brewer Fuller's.

34. THE ALBION, No. 10 Thornhill Road, N1

These days Islington is a busy and bustling place, but you don't have to stray too far off the beaten track to find little pockets of solitude and calm. Bits of Barnsbury are a case in point, and I dare say that when you stumble across the Albion for the first time a warm glow might very well descend upon you.

This, you see, is a pretty chocolate-box pub, a Regency-style flat-fronted building, late Georgian with a small porch over its main entrance and ivy and wisteria climbing up its front. The hectic Liverpool Road is only yards away, but choose your moment and a visit to The Albion can feel like a trip to an English country inn.

For much of the nineteenth century Islington was developed as a residential area. Until then, however, it was largely rolling fields, small hamlets and a number of noted pleasure gardens. Places like Barnsbury, and also Canonbury and Highbury, were popular destinations for Londoners seeking refuge from the crowded city, places where they could breathe fresh air and take the waters – perhaps even something a little stronger.

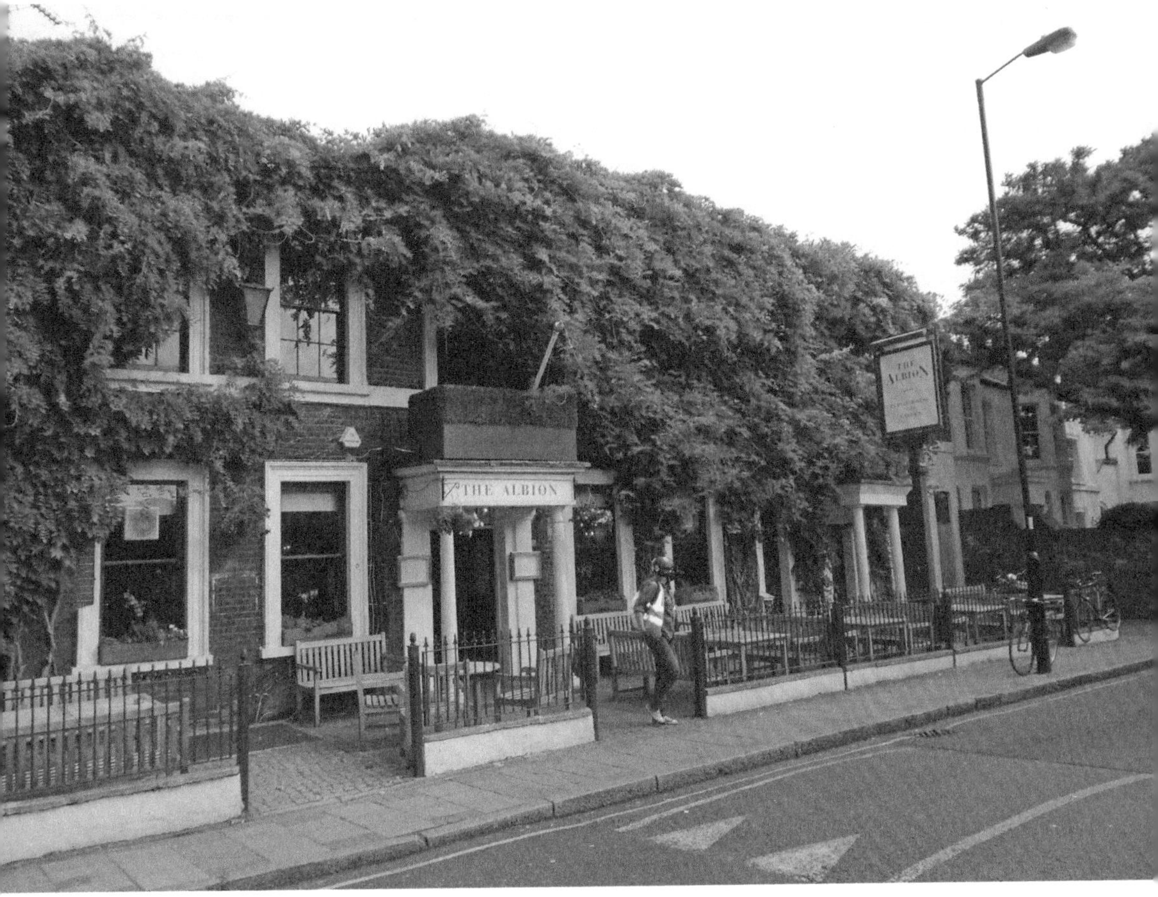

The Albion, Thornhill Road.

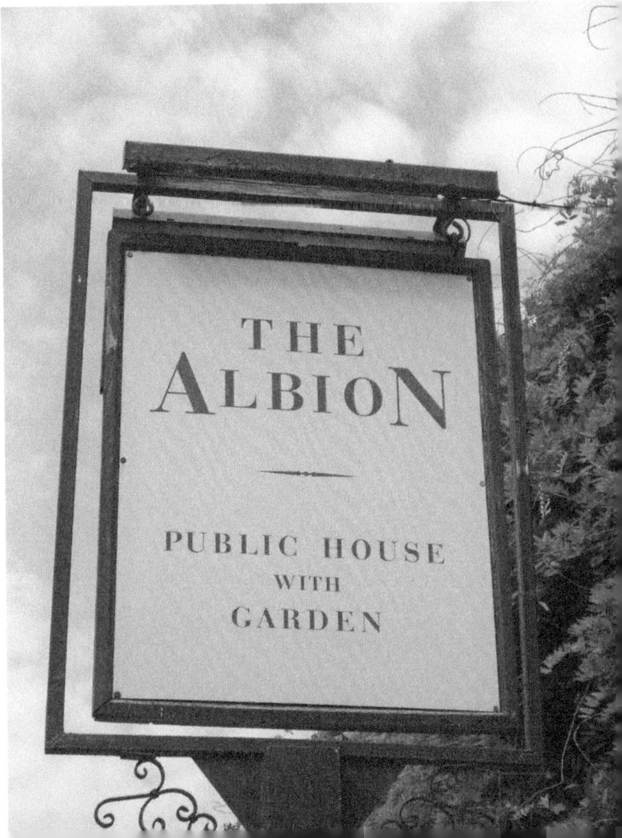

Cricket

The man we have to thank for what is now The Albion was one Thomas Albion Oldfield. He owned substantial land here, including a dairy, and to cater for the many revellers he opened the Albion teahouse, which in time morphed into today's pub.

Some accounts insist that The Albion was a coaching inn, but given that it wasn't on a coaching route, this is almost certainly not the case.

Oldfield also owned a field roughly where today's Barnsbury Road and Dewey Road meet. It was here, from the 1780s, that some of the very earliest games of organised cricket were played, notably by the aristocratic White Conduit Club, also known as the WCC. In June1885 a team representing the county of Kent were beaten here by the WCC, although only by five runs.

The matches attracted huge crowds, elements of which were famously rowdy in their behaviour, notably towards the gentlemen cricketers. A young WCC bowler called Thomas Lord was therefore tasked with looking for an alternative, more select venue, which he successfully did in 1787 when he secured 7 acres of land off Dorset Square, in what is now St John's Wood. The WCC promptly moved there and in time evolved into the Marylebone Cricket Club. The rest is history.

Today's Albion fancies itself as a rather upmarket gastropub. Its large back garden is one of the most attractive in London, although not quite big enough for a game of cricket.

35. THE CAMDEN HEAD, No. 2 Camden Walk, N1

Despite its elegant exterior and sumptuous, ever-so slightly seductive interior, do not be deceived by The Camden Head, for this pub, despite its airs and its graces, is a real survivor. It has managed to come through two world wars – and this stretch of Islington took delivery of its fair share of Luftwaffe bombs – and even endured the 1960s and 1970s.

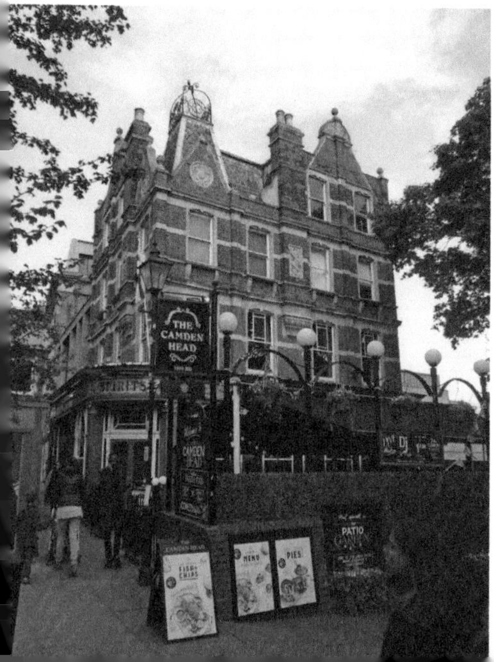

The Camden Head, Camden Walk.

It is this latter fact that is truly remarkable, for those two decades were brutal as far as pub preservation and conservation were concerned. Giant brewing and pub companies cared little for history and tradition, or for design aesthetics: for them a 100-year-old pane of etched gin palace glass was there to be smashed and replaced; a grand mahogany island bar was so much firewood.

In 1969 it was decided that The Camden Head was due a makeover. Although a pub has stood here since 1806, the current building dates from 1899, just as the great pub-building boom of the period ended. However at this point in time, the 1960s, similar pubs all over London, all over the country for that matter, were being gutted without thought and with even less ceremony. But Roderick Gradidge, who was given the task, had other ideas.

Victorian Values

Gradidge was a respected architect and writer on architecture, who for a period in the 1960s specialised in pub interiors. However he was also a leading member of the Victorian Society, a charity set up to protect Victorian and Edwardian architecture and design.

Working with what was left of the 1899 pub, he set about a sympathetic and quite astonishing restoration. All of which means that today's Camden Head, very much a gin palace in look and feel, still features some surviving glass panelling and mirrors, not to mention a magnificent island bar complete with original clock, by W. S. Pond of Clerkenwell.

The stained glass in the upstairs function room was rescued from a house undergoing demolition in Marlborough Crescent, Bedford Park. This upstairs space now hosts live

The Camden Head was restored in the late 1960s.

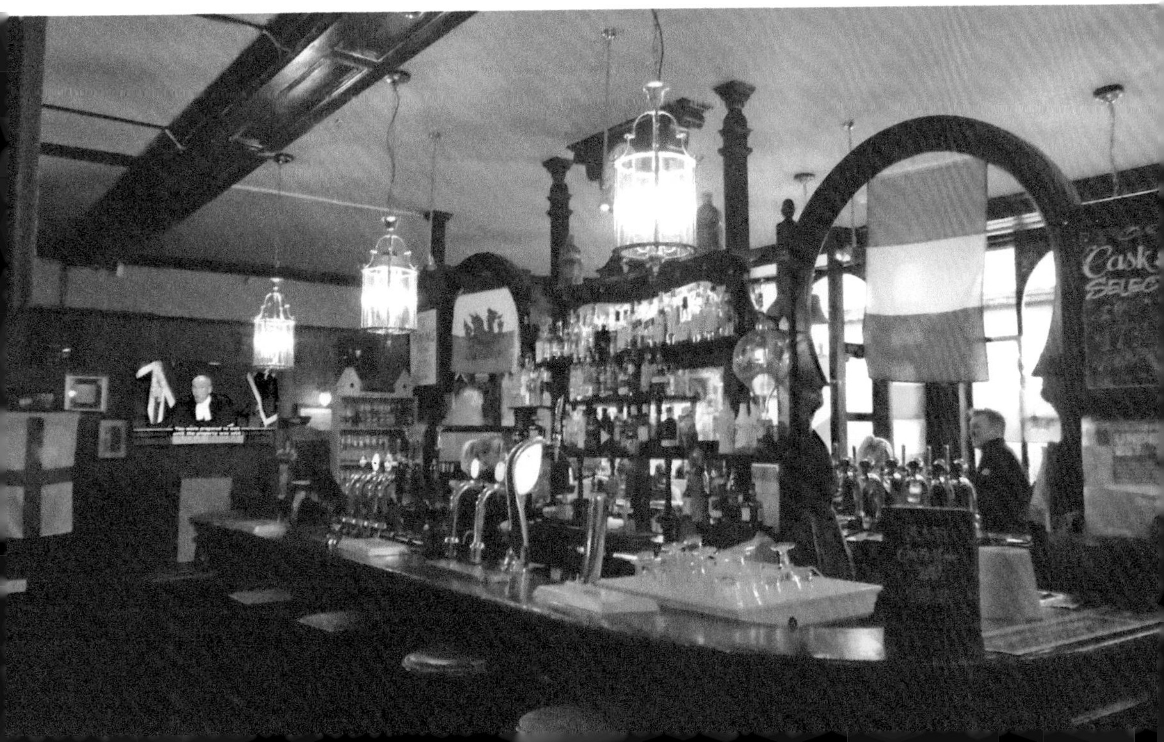

comedy nights, but during the pub's early (late) Georgian days was a 'birth-control clinic', most probably where prophylactics could be bought.

All things considered, it is no wonder the Camden Head enjoys Grade II status and the next time I pop by for a swift one I'll certainly raise a glass to Roderick Gradidge.

36. FOX ON THE GREEN, No. 1 Islington Green, N1

The Fox on the Green is an imposing Victorian pub located on the corner of Islington Green and Upper Street. A hostelry of one sort or another has stood here since at least 1802 – some sources suggest perhaps a little earlier – but the current rather handsome building dates from 1872 and is Grade II listed.

Over the years the pub has certainly reflected the changing fortunes and social make-up of Islington, which since the late 1960s has been transformed from a rundown and predominantly working-class district of London into one of the capital's most fashionable and desirable places to live.

The Fox, to give this pub its original name, was ideally located as a stop-off point for those approaching London from the north. Upper Street, feeding as it does St John Street headed south, has always been a busy thoroughfare and the scale upon which the pub was rebuilt in 1872 suggests that accommodation was available.

The Fox on the Green, thankfully no longer the Slug and Lettuce.

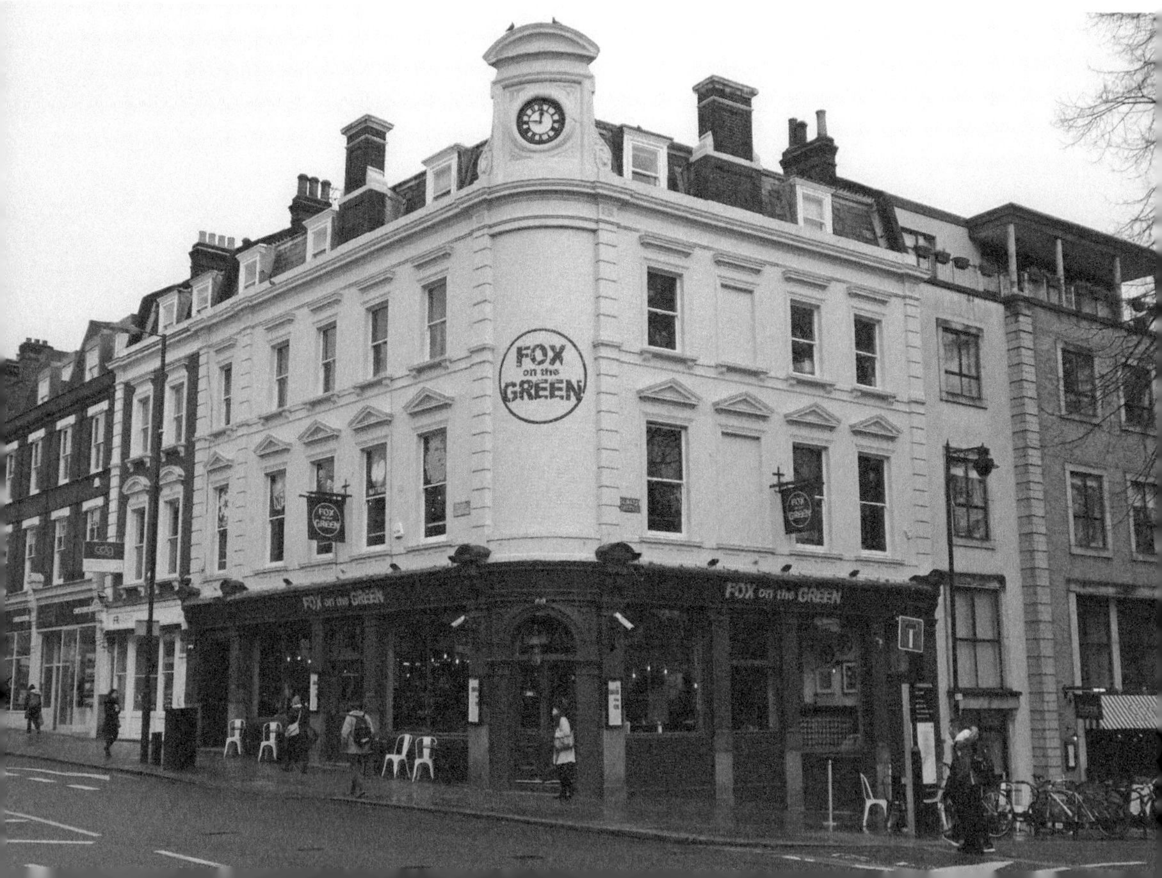

Slug and Lettuce

The bar of the Fox has always been a busy place. Collins Music Hall, one of north London's premiere temples of entertainment right up until 1958 when it closed following a catastrophic fire, was located just yards away and no doubt many a blue-nosed comic or cheerful chorus girl took a restorative nip of gin here.

It's hard to believe now, given how busy Upper Street is these days, but for much of the 1970s the thoroughfare was rundown and largely unloved. Many shops were vacant and many boarded up, while most of the street's many hostelries, including the Fox, were as shabby and worn out as many of their customers appeared to be.

In 1984, with gentrification of the area now well and truly underway, the Fox was transformed into the Slug and Lettuce, a pub clearly aimed broadly at Islington's new bright young things and more particularly at female customers. There are now more than seventy Slug and Lettuce pubs across the United Kingdom, but this Islington branch was the very first, the brainchild of hotel and hospitality veteran Hugh Corbett. The change of pub name, seemingly at the whim of people more interested in marketing than history, did not go down well with everyone.

I am pleased to report then that in April, 2016, following a lengthy makeover, the pub reopened as the Fox on the Green with at least part of its original name restored.

37. STEAM PASSAGE TAVERN, Nos 44–46 Upper Street, N1

Today's Steam Passage Tavern was briefly, from 1976 through to the mid-1980s, known as the Champion. The pub's original name, however, was the Star and Garter and there

Steam Passage Tavern, Upper Street.

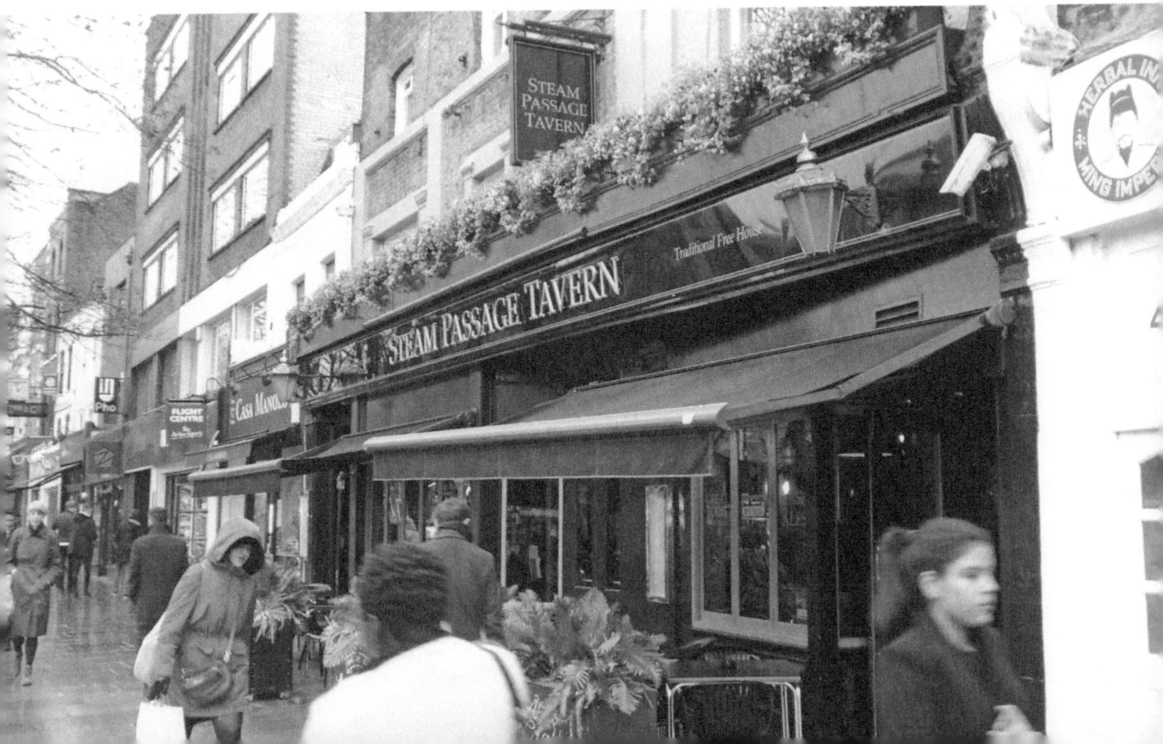

are records of it here on Upper Street as early as 1820, probably little more than an alehouse operating out of a private residence. A full tavern licence was obtained in 1831, and the Star and Garter was effectively born.

Star and Garter is not an uncommon pub name. It refers to the most noble Order of the Garter, which is the highest order of knighthood and third most important honour after the Victoria Cross and the George Cross. It was instigated by Edward II, around 1348, but is only open members of the royal family alongside just twenty-five knights.

In the days before sportsmen and women routinely became millionaires, it was not uncommon for retiring athletes to become publicans, and that's what happened at the Star and Garter in 1946 when Len Harvey became landlord.

Heavyweight Champion

Although originally from Cornwall, Harvey had moved to north London at the age of sixteen to pursue a career in professional boxing. This he did with great success, becoming British champion at three different weight divisions (middleweight, light-heavyweight and heavyweight) and British Empire champion at two (light-heavy and heavyweight).

A huge star in his heyday, in June 1934 some 90,000 packed into the old White City stadium to watch him defend his heavyweight title against Welshman Jack Stevensen. Harvey, with his poster-boy good looks, was also the first boxer to enter the ring wearing a dressing gown.

During the Second World War he joined the Royal Air Force. His last competitive bout was in June 1942, when he was knocked out by the younger Freddie Mills.

As landlord of the Star and Garter he was a popular figure and was still in charge in 1965 when Martin Green and Tony White's entertaining *Guide to London Pubs* was published. They seemed to like the pub, commending it for its 'good hot snacks' and also commenting on its clientele, which was 'local and passing, and includes old friends of the guvnor, whose personality unobtrusively dominates the atmosphere'. Harvey would have been fifty-eight at the time and was clearly still not a man to be messed with.

Harvey passed away in 1976, after which the pub's name was briefly changed to the Champion in his honour. Harvey's image can be found today occupying the back wall inside the Steam Tavern Passage. In an odd way it still feels as if he's the guvnor here.

38. OLD QUEEN'S HEAD, No. 44 Essex Road, N1

Today The Old Queen's Head is a hip hangout for Islington's beautiful people, but scratch a little beneath the surface and you will discover a very old pub with a fascinating history.

A tavern has stood on this site since the early seventeenth century, although the current pub dates from around 1830 with a frontage of around 1900. This still makes it one of the area's oldest surviving hostelries and it remains a handsome old building with a touch of late Georgian elegance about. It has been Grade II listed since 1954.

Until its demolition in 1829, 'to the regret of all antiquaries' according to that great chronicler of London Walter Thornbury in his epic *Old London* of 1873, The Old Queen's Head was a noted tavern, a gabled building of 'three lofty storeys, projecting over each other in front, and forming bay windows, supported by brackets and carved figures'.

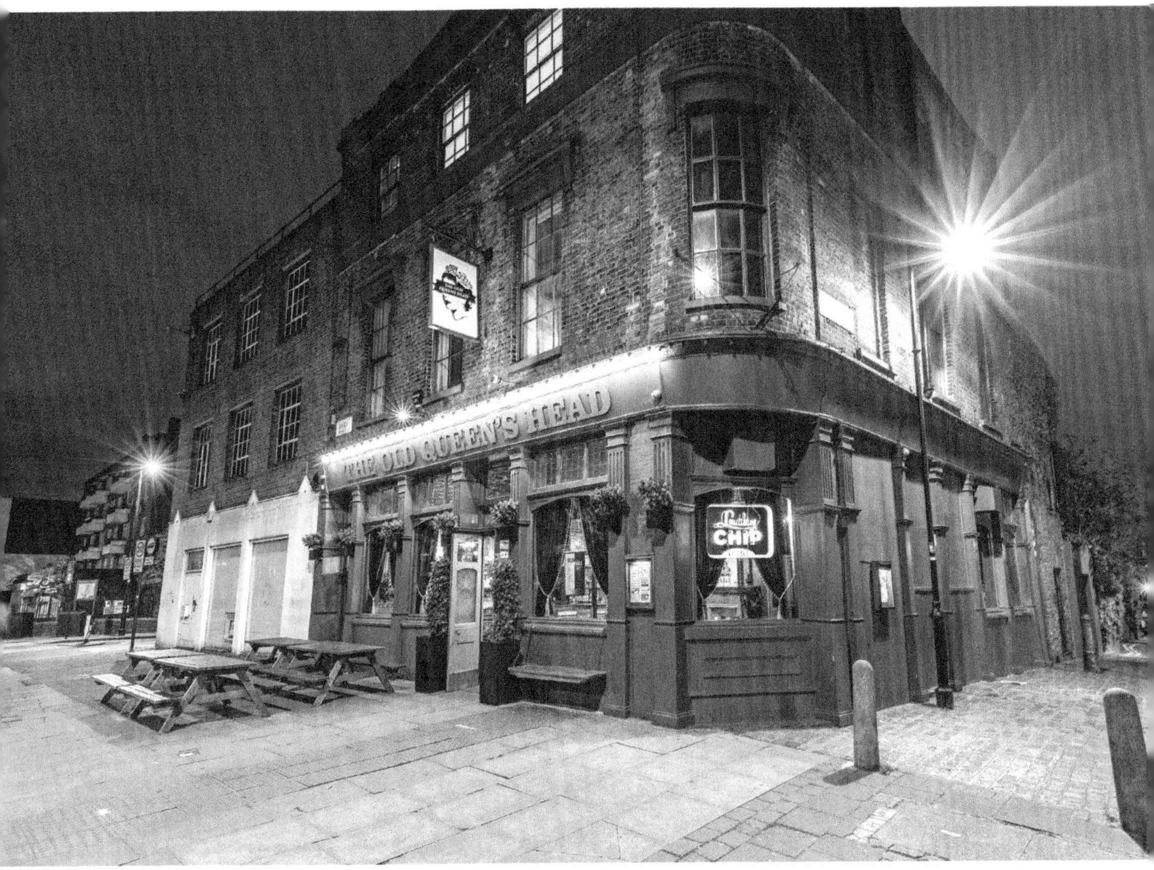

The Old Queen's Head, Essex Road.

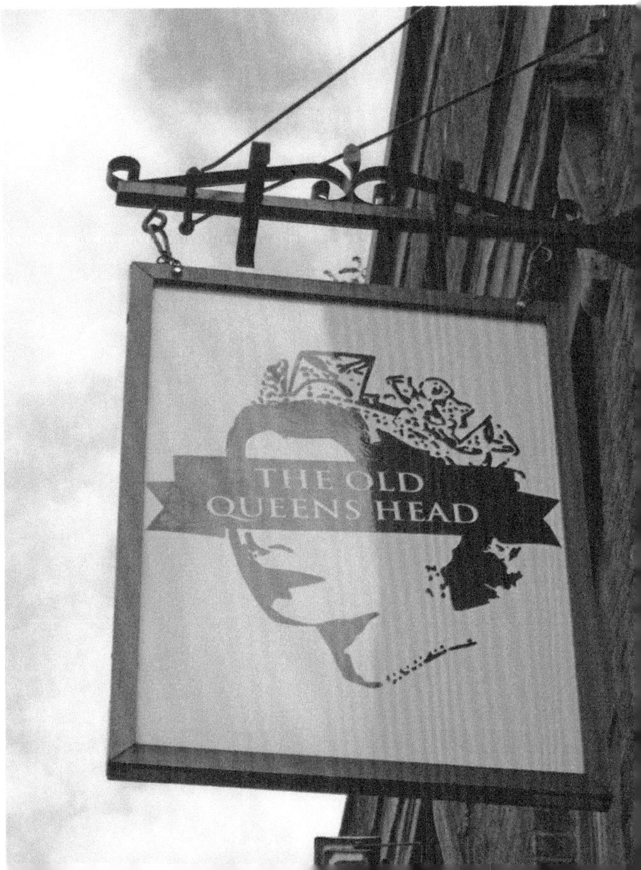

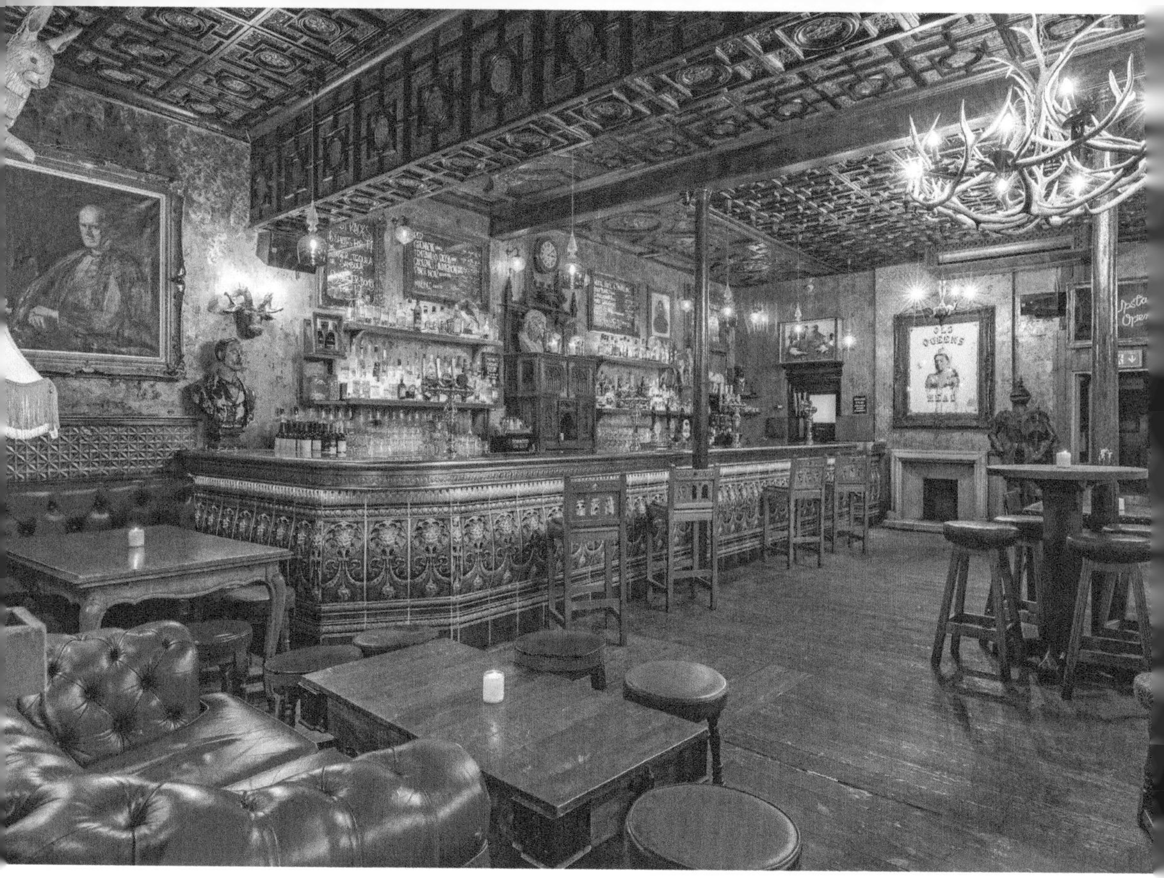

Above: Inside the Old Queen's Head.

Below: Rare seventeenth-century fireplace, with detail, from The Old Queen's Head.

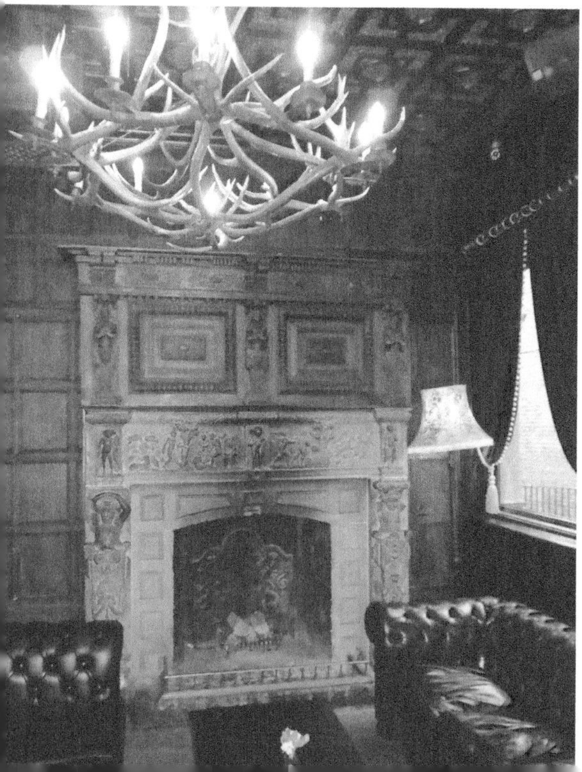

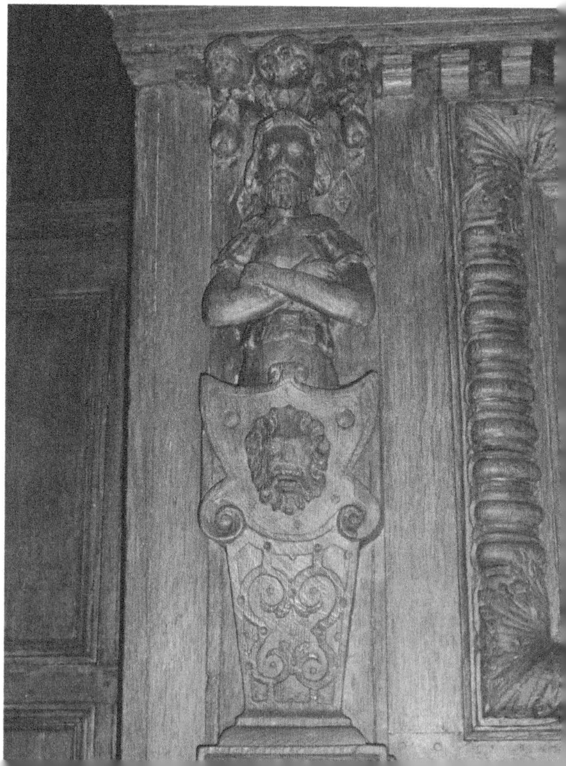

Remarkable Interior

Although the pulling down of the old pub caused much consternation, some of the old interior fixtures and fittings were retained, most notably the magnificent fireplace, made of stone and wood, which is of seventeenth-century origin and features some intricate and ornate carvings depicting, according to Thornbury, 'the stories of Danae and Actaeon, in relief, with mutilated figures of Venus, Bacchus and Plenty'.

A little battered in places, it purports to be the 'oldest working fireplace in north London', and to this day is often lit when the temperature demands it. The fireplace, not to mention parts of the ceiling which feature model plasterwork and are reckoned in places to also be seventeenth century, forms part of a remarkable pub interior that incorporates the old and the contemporary for an overall feel that might best be described as twenty-first-century Gothic.

The pub has long been associated with Sir Walter Raleigh, though there is little hard fact to back this association and claims that he actually resided here have never been proved, although the great Elizabethan polymath certainly did live in Islington for a time. His residence eventually became the Pied Bull inn nearby, which sadly is no longer with us.

What we do know for sure is that for a while during the reign of Elizabeth I Raleigh enjoyed a 'patent' giving him the power to grant licences for the 'keeping of taverns and retailing of wines throughout England'. For a fee, naturally. It seems likely that The Old Queen's Head was among the earliest inns to be granted such a licence, and to mark the occasion named itself in honour of Good Queen Bess.

39. KING'S HEAD, No. 115 Upper Street, N1

For many post-war years, like many Islington hostelries, the King's Head had fallen on hard times. The paint and plaster were peeling from this grand old Victorian structure, built 1864, and the customers were few and far between.

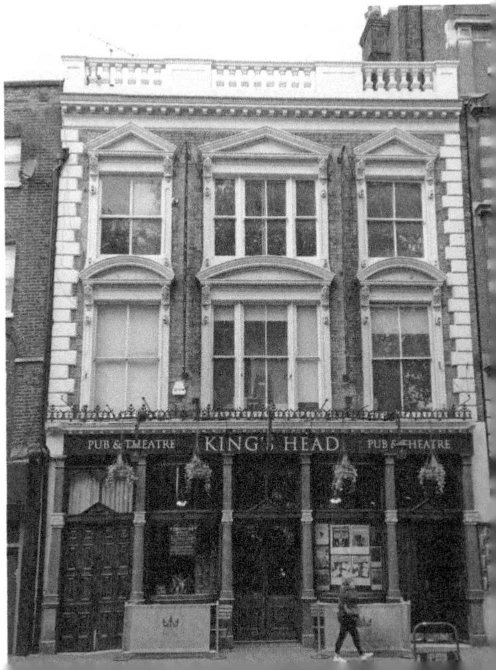

The King's Head, Upper Street.

Enter stage left, in 1970, ex-pat American Dan Crawford. He had arrived in England the year before from Hackensack, New Jersey, and harboured the dream of establishing the concept of dinner theatre in London. What he also seems to have done, perhaps inadvertently, is help create fringe theatre in the capital and revive theatrical performances in a pub setting, which hadn't really been done since Shakespeare's day.

There has been a King's Head tavern here since 1543, named after Henry VIII, and it is one of Islington's oldest surviving pubs. It also has another royal link for in 1603, on his way to the Charterhouse in Clerkenwell to prepare for his coronation, James I stopped off here en route.

The old King's Head was also popular with Samuel Pepys. The great diarist knew it affectionately as 'the cheese-cake house' and visited often. The 'cheese-cake' that he refers to, incidentally, was a type of spiced curd tart.

In a diary entry dated 25 April 1664, Pepys wrote: 'And thence back to Islington and at the King's head [sic], where Pitts lived, and we light and eat and drunk for remembrance of the old house sake.' Pitts was landlord of the King's Head.

Theatre

When Crawford and his second wife Joan took over the pub in 1969, they did so with funds totalling just £1,100. The back room, a billiards hall that had also housed a

Main bar of the King's Head, Upper Street.

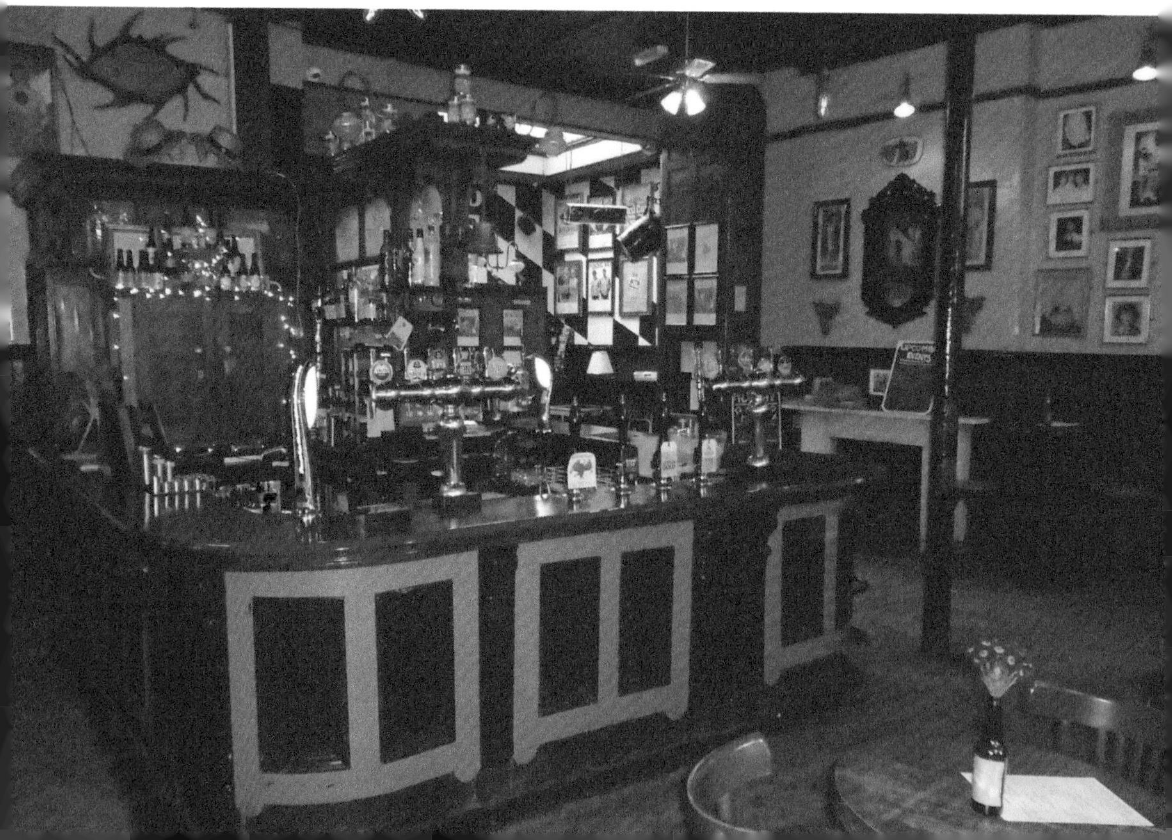

boxing rink, was transformed into a basic theatre space with the emphasis very much on the basic. The pub had not been decorated since 1938. On the pub theatre's opening night in December, 1970 – a production of *The Empire Builders* by Boris Vian – the Crawford's had a float of just £15 to play with.

In the years since, the venue has staged a number of award-winning productions and some of the great and good of English theatre have performed here during their salad days, among them John Hurt, Ben Kingsley, Anthony Sher, Tom Conti, Ray Winstone and, er, Christopher Biggins.

The pub has existed hand to mouth for many years and closure has loomed on a number of occasions. However goodwill and benefit performances, in particular from the late Victoria Wood, have kept the place going. Although Crawford died in July 2005, the theatre still thrives and the pub remains reassuringly scruffy. Alas, the custom of charging for drinks in pre-decimal money no longer continues, although the rather grand old Edwardian till remains.

40. HOPE & ANCHOR, No. 207 Upper Street, N1

For people of a certain age and musical disposition, the Hope & Anchor is as important a part of London's rock and roll heritage as the Abbey Road zebra crossing immortalised by the Beatles or the Heddon Street telephone box in which David Bowie posed as Ziggy Stardust.

Today's pub is a sturdy late Victorian street corner affair. It was built in 1880, although records show that a public house, probably little more than a beer shop, stood here as early as the 1830s.

The Hope & Anchor was one of London's seminal live music venues.

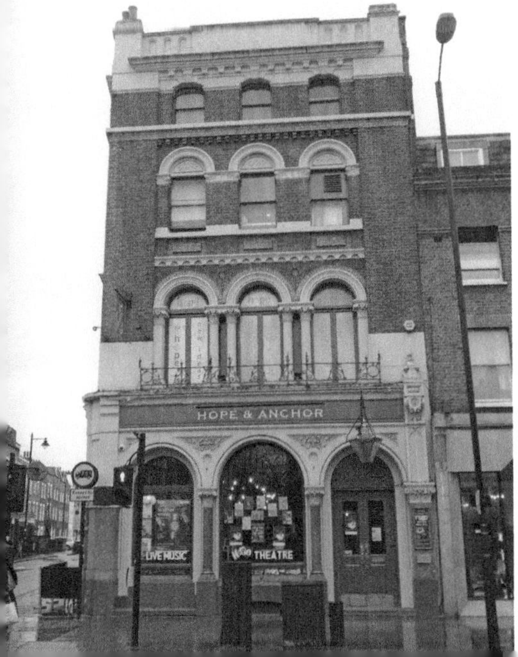

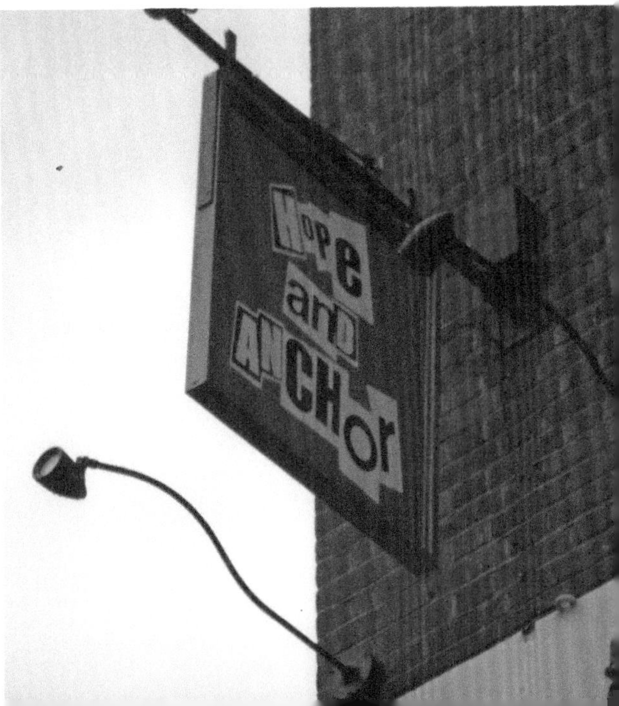

The pub survived the fluctuating fortunes of Upper Street – decidedly down on its luck until gentrification changed the face of Islington – and in the early 1970s, almost by accident, became one of the capital's most important live music venues.

Pub rock was a back-to-basics, rough and ready style of music with its heartland in north London. When the Tally Ho, Kentish Town, one of its best-known venues, changed its entertainment policy to instead embrace traditional Irish music, the Hope & Anchor, managed by Fred Grainger and Dave Robinson, was transformed into a pub rock Mecca. Robinson would later set up the Stiff Records label.

Festival Album

At the beginning of 1976 John Eichler took over as landlord and the pub entered a golden age. Over the next few years its cramped and smoky basement hosted a number of acts that would go on to achieve greatness, artistically and sometimes commercially too.

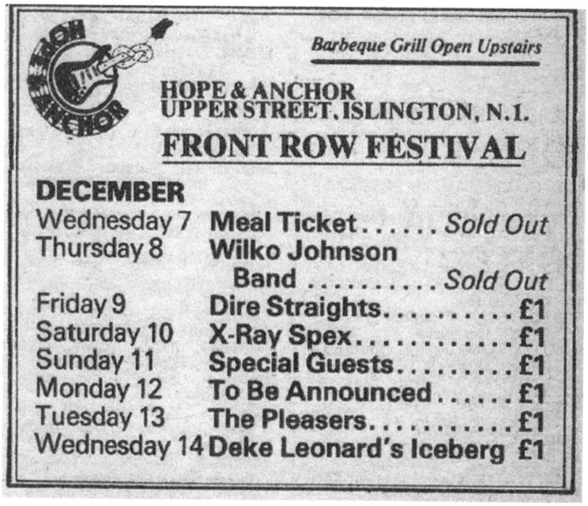

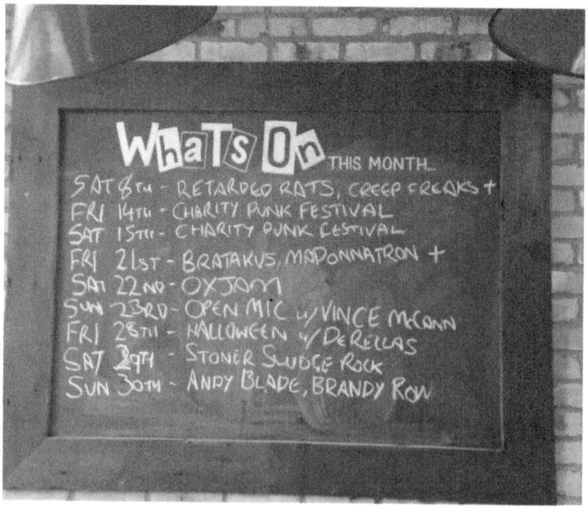

Advertisement for 1977's famous Front Row festival. The pub is still a live music venue.

A vast and varied roster has appeared over the years, including Joy Division, who made their London debut here in December 1978, and U2, in December 1979, billed as 'V2'. The Jam played some of their earliest shows here, as did the Police, Squeeze, Adam and The Ants and Madness, to name just a few.

Throughout November and December 1977 the pub staged the Front Row Festival, featuring a number of well-known pub rock and punk acts of the time. A double live album, culled from the shows, was released the following year with performances from, among others, the Stranglers, XTC, Dire Straits (mistakenly billed pre-festival as Dire 'Straights'), X-Ray Spex and the Wilko Johnson Band.

The pub closed in the early 1980s, falling derelict. For a brief time it became a squat and, although no longer licensed, staged a number of chaotic live shows featuring anarcho-punk bands such as Conflict.

Organised concerts returned to the venue, by now again a pub, in 1996. These days it's owned by Suffolk brewer and pub company Greene King. Alas the sticky carpet and weary wallpaper of old has gone, replaced by bench seating, bare wooden floors and sadly stripping the place of much of its louche pub rock charm. But at least live music survives in the famous cellar.

Inside & Hope and Anchor, Upper Street.

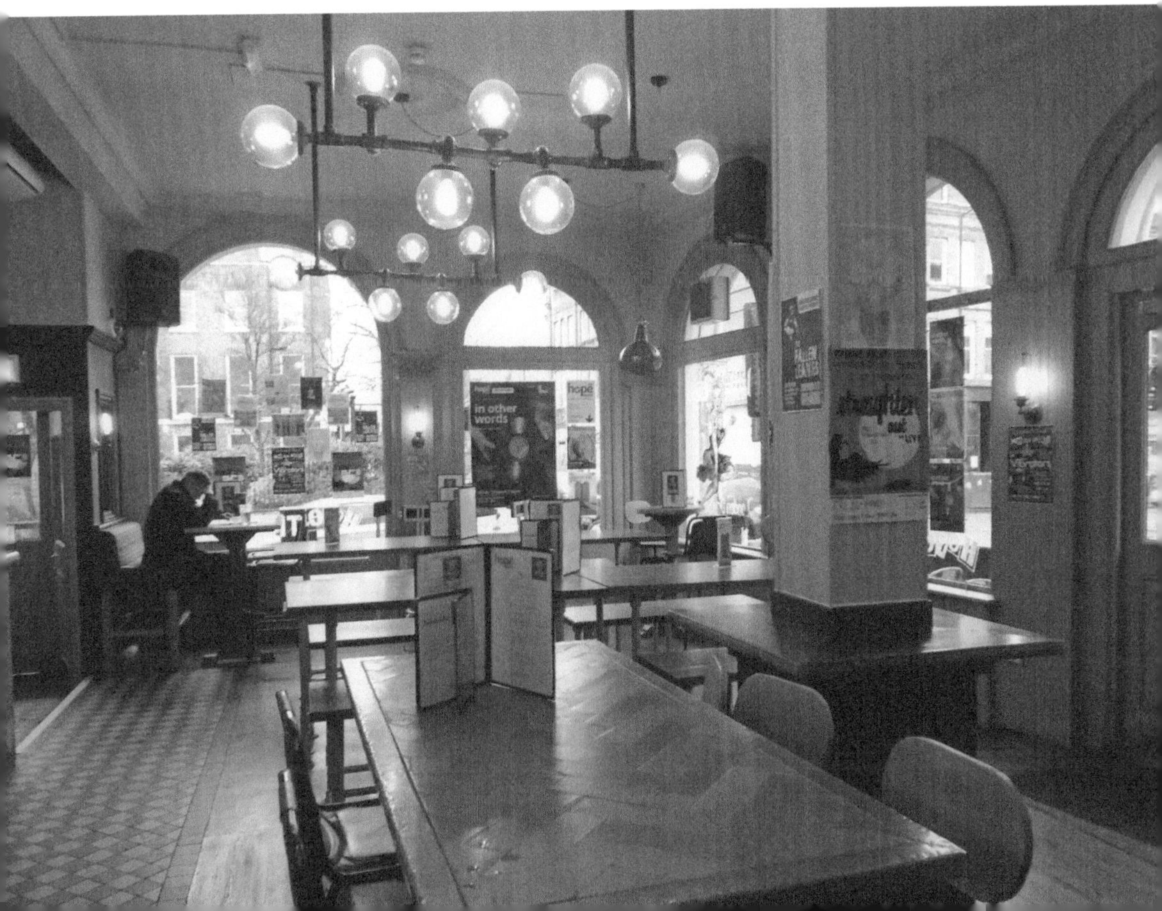

4

Highbury, Holloway and Islington North

41. HIGHBURY BARN, No. 26 Highbury Park, N5

Today's Highbury Barn pub owes its very existence to the London pleasure garden boom of the eighteenth century and a time when most of Islington offered rolling green fields and fresh air to the denizens of the crowded City to the south.

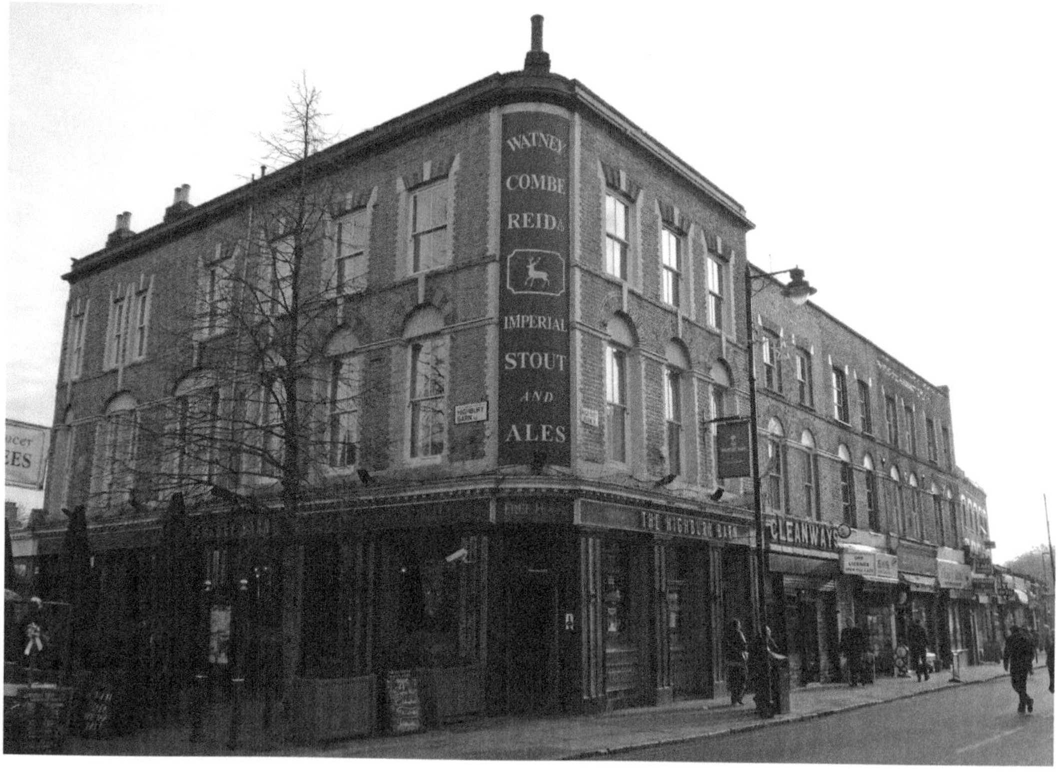

The Highbury Barn, Highbury Park.

This part of north London was once the manor of the Priors of St John but by 1740 was a popular destination for Londoners venturing into the 'country' and a tea garden was established in a former farm building. By 1762 it had evolved into a 'cake and alehouse', known as Willoughby's. The playwright Oliver Goldsmith was a regular visitor.

As more and more people visited the attraction grew in size and sophistication. By 1811, the Highbury Barn Assembly House boasted ornate gardens and a bowling green. By the mid-nineteenth century it was operating on a grand scale and in 1841 more than 3,000 attended the annual dinner of the licensed victuallers association.

Rise and Fall

In 1854 the Barn staged an ascent by the English balloonist Charles Green and four years later the venue was turned into a grand concert hall. Over the next decade such celebrated artists as tightrope walker Blondin, the gymnast Leotard and the famous Siamese twins appeared.

In 1861 Edward Giovanelli took over the licence and in 1865 rebuilt the Barn as a music hall called the Alexandra Theatre. This seems to have marked both a brief golden age for the Barn but also its demise.

The venue had became known for its 'riotous and bawdy' customers and matters came to a head in 1869 when drunken students from St Bartholomew's Hospital started a 'nearriot'. In 1871 Giovanelli was refused a new dancing and alcohol licence and the venue promptly closed.

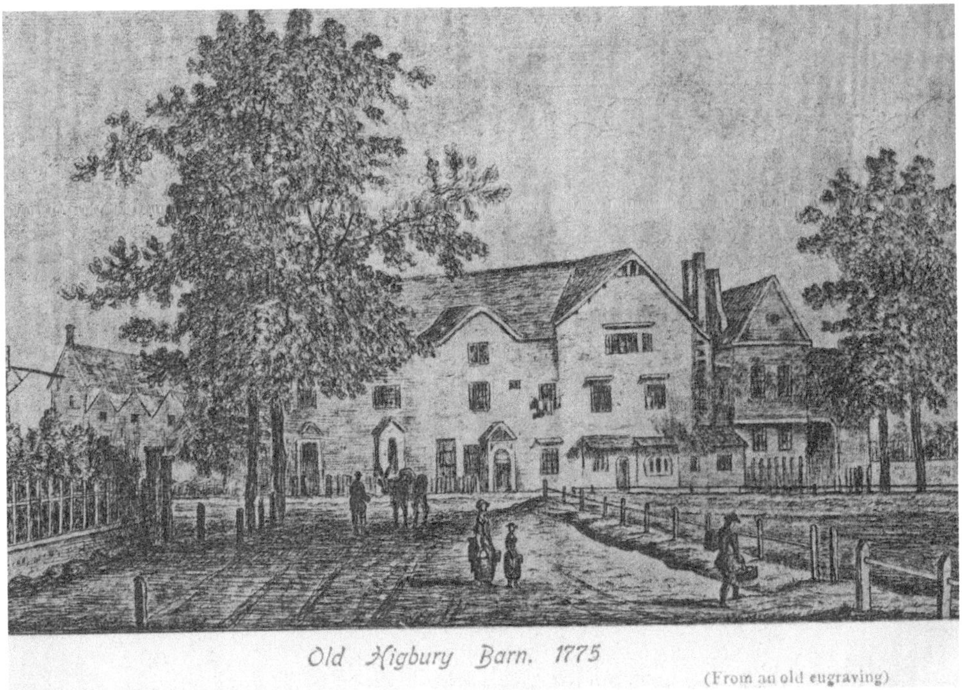

Highbury Barn from a seventeenth-century engraving.

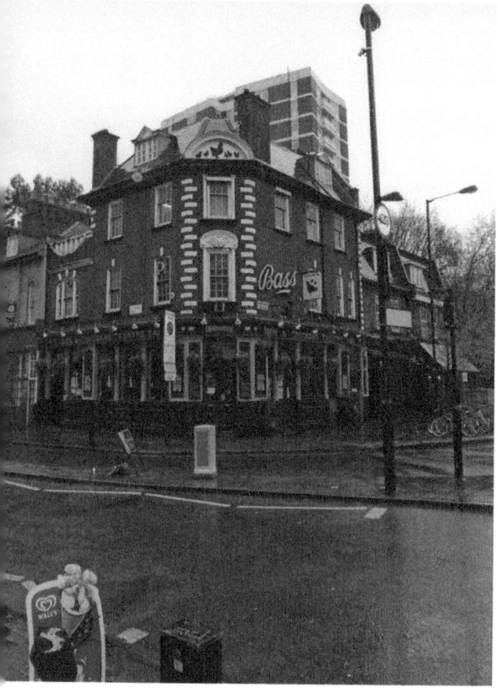

The Hen and Chickens, St Paul's Road.

Today's Highbury Barn pub was opened in 1885 and sits on part of the pleasure garden site. It was built for the famous London brewer Watney Combe Reid, and their name can still be seen on today's exterior (although it was for a time painted over).

Inside it has been given a rather bland makeover but there are some ornate iron pillars that have survived. It gets very, very busy when the Arsenal are playing at home. Their Emirates Stadium is a short stroll away.

The Barn is also a pub with a plaque, an 'Islington People's Plaque' no less. It reminds us that the Peasants' Revolt of 1381 reached this then rural area of north London. The plaque tells us that 'Highbury Manor was burnt and destroyed.' It probably seemed like a good idea at the time.

42. HEN & CHICKENS, No. 109 St Paul's Road, N1

The Hen & Chickens is one of a handful of pubs in Islington that can claim a connection with George Orwell. Between 1944 and 1947 the great writer lived nearby at No. 27b Canonbury Square. Today the address is marked by a plaque, unveiled by Orwell's adopted son Richard in May 2016.

Orwell was clearly fond of his pint and in addition to propping up the bar at the Hen & Chickens was also a regular at a number of other pubs in the area, most notably the Canonbury Tavern and the Compton Arms. Although best known for his novels, Orwell was also an accomplished journalist and essayist and one of his most famous pieces was a column written for the *London Evening Standard* in 1946 about his idea of what constituted the perfect pub. This 'perfect' pub was given the fictitious name of the Moon Under Water, but, reality often proving more far-fetched than fiction, a number of pubs run by the JD Wetherspoon chain have in recent years adopted the name, although I doubt any of them feature the 'uncompromisingly Victorian' fittings that Orwell insisted upon, or for that matter barmaids who 'know the customers by name'.

Nineteen Eighty-Four

It seems, then, almost certain that the Hen & Chickens influenced Orwell's perfect pub ideal and if the great man returned today he would no doubt be pleased to see some surviving late Victorian features, although the live music would not have pleased him quite so much.

For many years the Hen & Chicken was owned by Charrington, one of London's most famous brewers who operated from the famous old Anchor Brewery in the Mile End Road, and it is possible that this also had an influence on the seminal *Nineteen Eighty-Four*, Orwell's best-known work.

One of the seemingly minor characters in *1984* is a junk shop owner who Winston Smith, the book's main protagonist, confides in. Unfortunately for Smith the junk shop owner is a Thought Police informant. His name is Charrington.

There's been a pub here, close to busy Highbury Corner, since 1865. The current building looks a little later and has some nice exterior features such as the plaster mother hen with her chicks and a huge sign proclaiming 'Bass'. The Hen & Chickens, like several other hostelries in this neck of the woods, is a leading exponent of pub theatre.

43. THE COMPTON ARMS, No. 4 Compton Avenue, N1

Just yards from the hustle and bustle of Upper Street, one of Islington's main arteries, you'll find Compton Avenue, positively sedate by comparison. And here you will find

The Compton Arms, Compton Avenue.

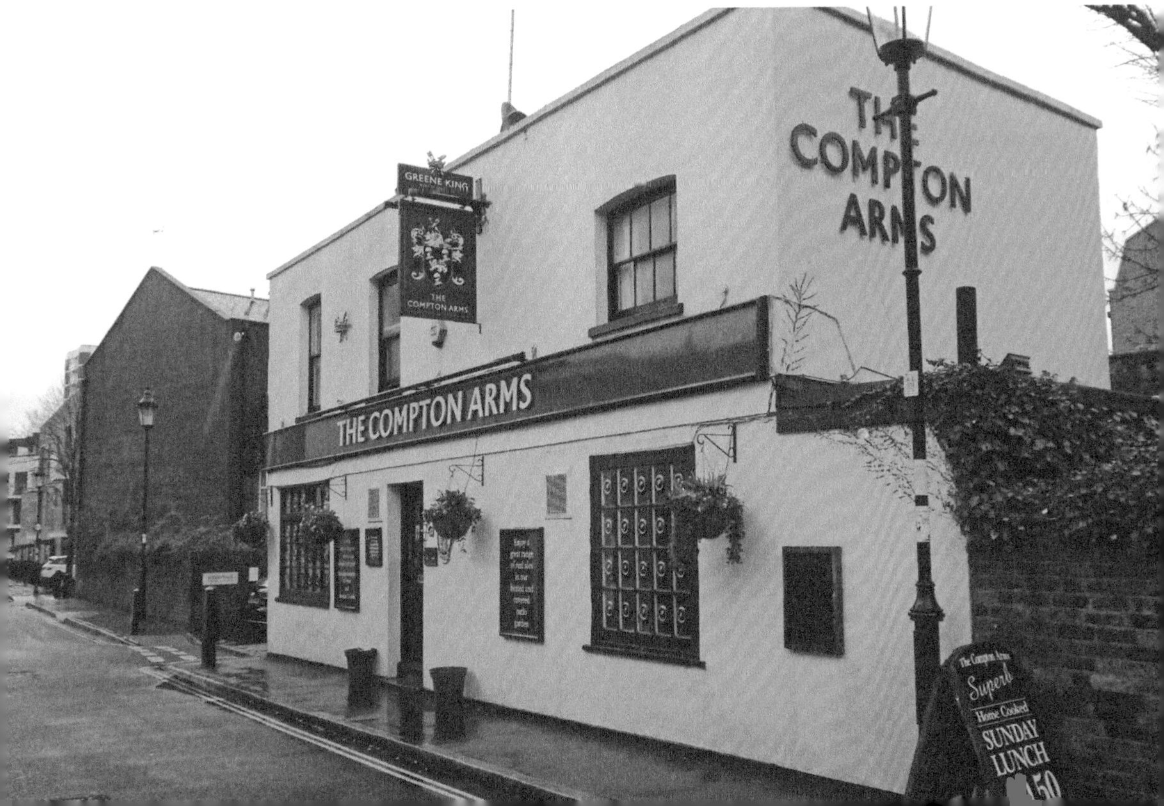

The Compton Arms, a small and intimate hostelry that has the air of a slightly down at heel country pub about it.

The pub, and Compton Avenue, are named after the ancient and aristocratic Compton family, earls of Northampton and for centuries the owners of vast tracts of land in Islington and Clerkenwell.

There are somewhat hazy records of a beerhouse on this site as early as the eighteenth century and The Compton Arms was certainly trading by the 1880s. Compton Avenue was essentially a mews to facilitate the grand houses of Compton Terrace just around the corner facing Upper Street, and the pub is small, modest in dimensions and quite humble in appearance.

It features a long bar to the front and a smaller back room. It is popular with supporters of the Arsenal, who play at the nearby Emirates, and the walls are a gallery to the Gunners.

George Orwell

Immediately before and after the Second World War Canonbury was a shabby district, bomb damaged but with vague aspiration of gentility. Gentrification came in the 1960s. Between 1944 and 1947 George Orwell lived in a flat just around the corner and a blue plaque marks the site at No. 27 Canonbury Square (Orwell resided at No. 27b).

Orwell loved pubs and beer, and was a regular at several local hostelries, most notably the Hen & Chickens, the Canonbury Tavern and the Compton Arms, which in the post-war years was also frequented by the likes of Arthur Koestler, Malcolm Muggeridge, John Betjeman and, later in the 1960s, Joe Orton.

Although most famous for works such as *Nineteen Eighty-Four* and *Animal Farm*, Orwell was also an accomplished essayist and journalist. In a 1946 piece for the *London Evening Standard* he wrote of his ideal of the perfect pub, giving it the fictitious name of the Moon Under Water.

Among the qualities he espoused were the absence of both radio and piano, barmaids 'who know the customers by name and take an interest in everyone' and 'fittings' which 'must be uncompromisingly Victorian'. In part at least the Moon Under Water was clearly inspired by the Compton and even though most of the pub's original Victoriana has sadly gone, I suspect that if Orwell walked through the door today he'd feel right at home.

44. THE CANONBURY TAVERN, No. 21 Canonbury Place, N1

The historic Islington enclave of Canonbury is just minutes from the traffic chaos of Highbury Corner and Holloway Road and yet, somehow, manages to retain a distinctly village feel. This is one of London's most exclusive neighbourhoods, affluent and for people with very deep pockets, so it seems only fitting that at its centre stands the Canonbury Tavern, a suitably well-heeled hostelry.

Canonbury can trace its origins to the mid-thirteenth century when the land was granted to the canons of St Bartholomew's Priory. When Henry VIII dissolved the priory in 1539, the manor was bestowed to Thomas Cromwell before changing ownership several times.

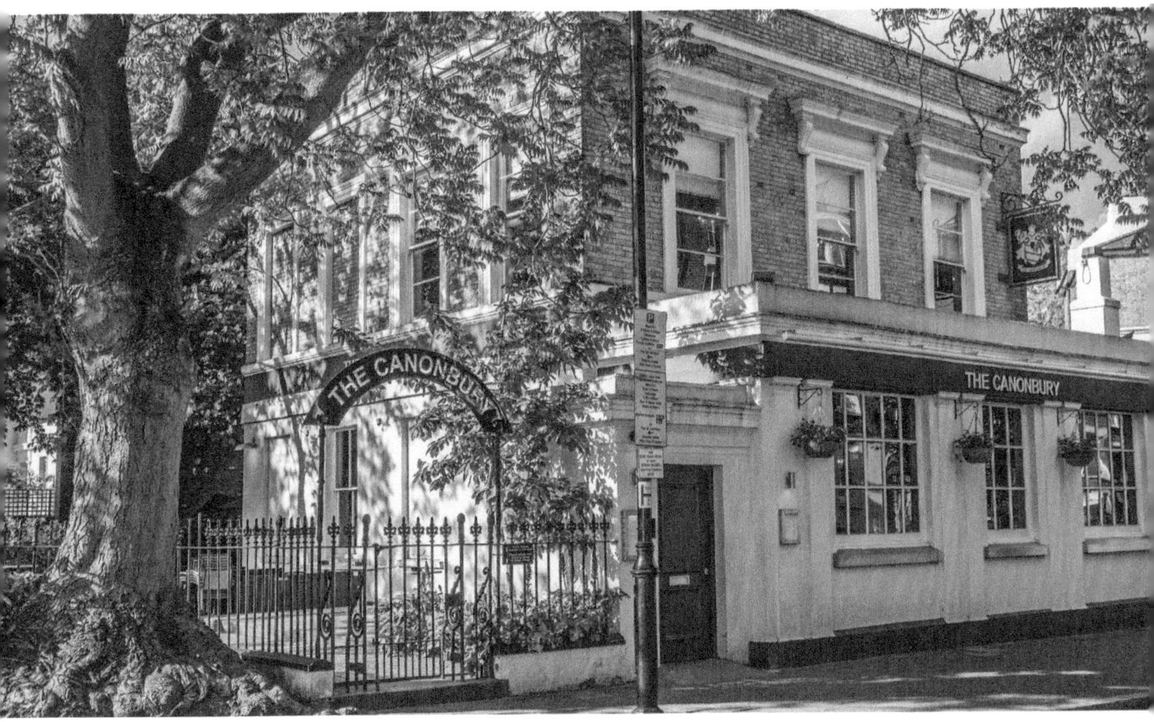

The Canonbury Tavern.

A hostelry of one sort or another has occupied this site since at least the seventeenth century, originally as old farm buildings converted into a crude alehouse enclosed by some of the ancient manorial walls.

It grew over the years to cater to the many visitors who would journey here for the clean air of then rural Canonbury, and was known, according to John Nelson writing in 1811's *History, Topography and Antiquities of The Parish of Islington,* for offering 'a beautiful aspect over the fields towards Hackney, Limehouse, etc [sic]'.

Grand Gardens

Around 1760 it was run by Benjamin Collins, a local churchwarden. It then changed hands several times, owned by, among others, a former soldier called James Lane who developed it substantially.

It was famed for its extensive gardens, covering 4 acres at one point. A later owner, Mr Sutton, laid out a bowling green and, according to Nelson, the grounds housed 'Dutch pin and trap ball yards, and a butt for the exercise of ball firing, which has of late been much resorted to by volunteers and others from the Metropolis'.

Evelyn Waugh was a regular here; he lived nearby between 1928 and 1930, and in the pub's famous gardens a few years later George Orwell would sit and write. Popular literary legend has it that parts of *Nineteen Eighty-Four* were penned beneath a chestnut tree here. Both men are commemorated by a gallery of pictures and images adorning one wall.

The current building dates from 1846 and had part of its upper floors removed in 1950 following either a fire or dry rot, depending on which story you choose to believe. Either way, today's pub can boast a staircase that literally leads nowhere.

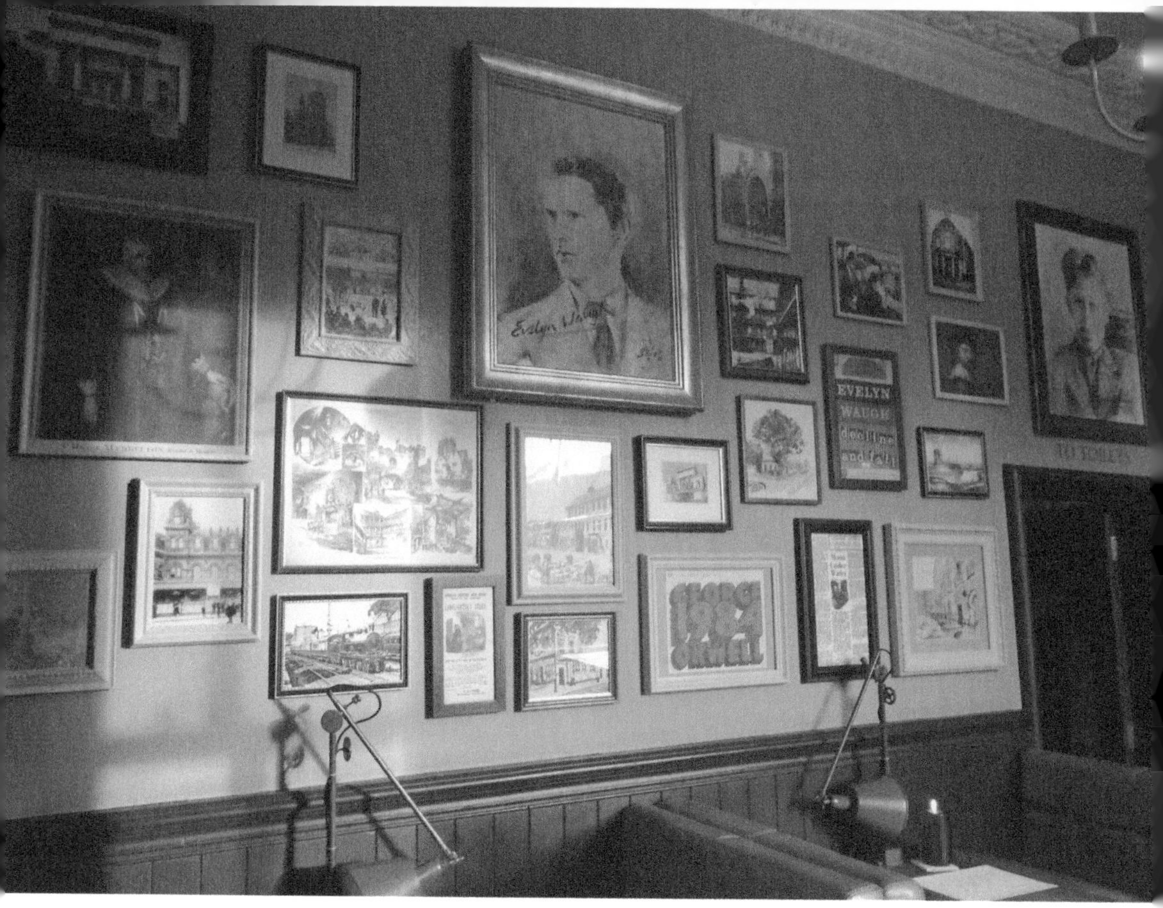

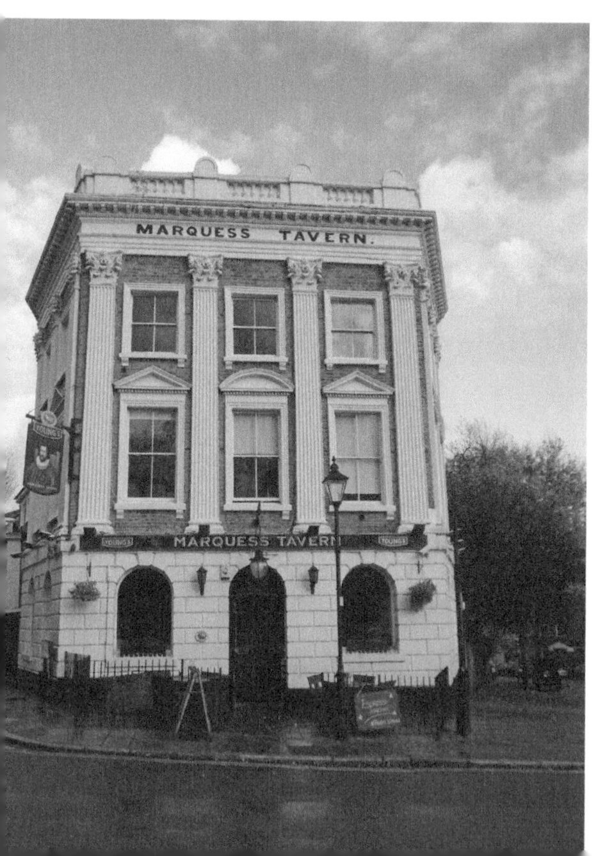

Above: Former regulars Orwell and Waugh are honoured inside the Canonbury Tavern.

Left: The Marquess Tavern, Canonbury.

For many years, until 2009, it stood empty and plans were afoot to convert it into residential use. Fortunately Lord Northampton, whose family own most of modern-day Canonbury, decreed that it should remain a pub. Well done Lord Northampton.

45. THE MARQUESS TAVERN, No. 32 Canonbury Street, N1

The Marquess Tavern rather creeps up on the casual perambulator. One moment you are wandering the leafy and well-heeled streets of Canonbury, quietly admiring the wealth of spectacular Georgian and Victorian town houses, and suddenly you turn a corner and there it is, the magnificent Grade II-listed Marquess Tavern in all its glory.

Built during the 1860s, and taking its name from the Marquess of Northampton whose family still own much of the land around these parts, it is both an imposing and grand construction complete with Corinthian pillars emanating from a stucco base. Its location, facing Canonbury Street but with extensive elevations along both Arran Walk and Douglas Road, make it a focal point, both geographically and socially, for the neighbourhood.

It is likely that much of the upper floors originally offered accommodation and those staying here could probably be sure of a good night's sleep. Although busy and noisy Essex Road is only yards away as the crow flies, this particular pocket of north London verges on the pastoral and the gentle trickle of what is left of the New River, a groundbreaking development of the early seventeenth century designed to bring clean water to London from rural Hertfordshire, can still be heard on tranquil summer evenings.

Unique Pub Sign

In 1979 the Marquess was acquired by the London brewer Young's, once famously of Wandsworth, and they did a painstaking job of restoring the old place to its

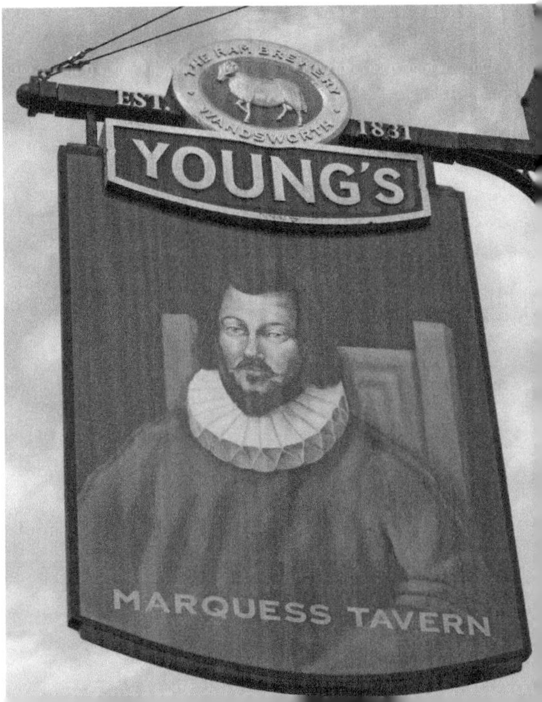

The Marquess Tavern.

former Victorian glory. But when they decided to put it on the market in 2008 some uncertainty over its future emerged.

However this is a story with a happy ending, for a group of five Canonbury residents united and, determined that their local would not be turned into yet another development of luxury apartments, took over ownership and moulded it into the pub we have today – undeniably upmarket and quite clearly of the gastro persuasion, with most of the serious eating taking place in a glass-canopied room to the rear that was once most likely a games rooms. There's no bar billiards or darts here now, alas.

The Marquess Tavern can also boast one of London's more unique hanging pub signs. From the front elevation it depicts a rather haughty-looking man, a Marquess of Northampton of old one assumes, sitting in a rather grand high-backed chair. If you can be bothered to check out the other side of the same sign, you'll find a rear view of the same man – which is to say the back of his head. Well, it made me smile.

46. THE MYDDLETON ARMS, No. 52 Canonbury Road, N1

The King's Head in Upper Street is most likely named in honour of Henry VIII while the Queen's Head in Essex Road after Elizabeth I, but it could be argued that Sir Hugh Myddelton, after whom this cosy little Canonbury pub is named, did more for London and Londoners than either of the aforementioned monarchs.

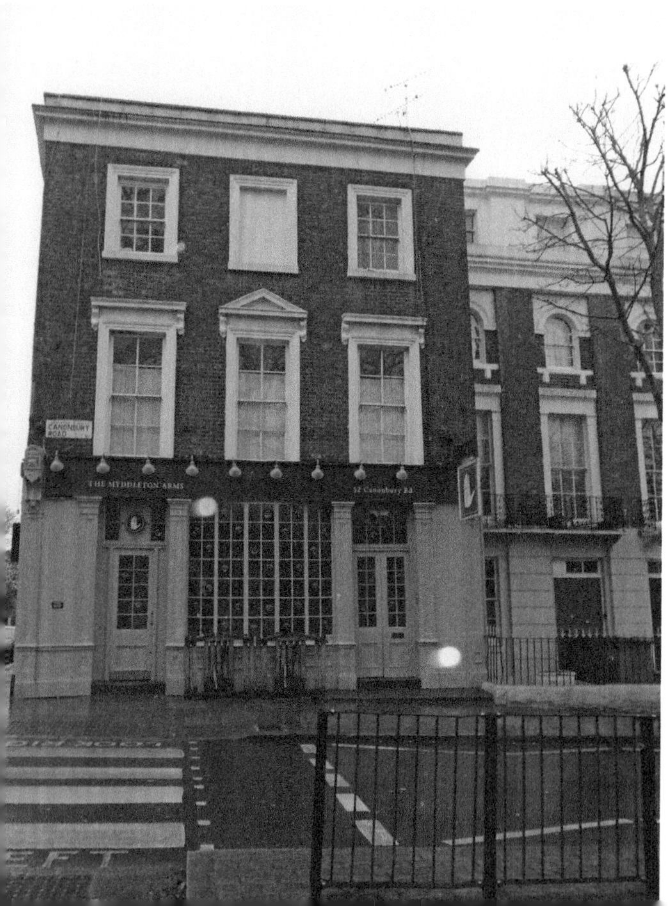

The Myddleton Arms, Canonbury Road.

At the start of the seventeenth century London was a rapidly growing city with an increasing population, but the continued lack of clean and safe drinking water was an ongoing problem. So around 1600 an ingenious plan was thought up by William Inglebert, namely to bring clean water from Amwell and St Chad's well in Ware, Hertfordshire, to the very heart of the capital. Inglebert favoured a covered 'vault of brick', but a West Country man by the name Edmund Colthurst instead suggested an open trench.

Acts of Parliament to undertake the task were granted to Colthurst in 1606 and to Inglebert in 1607. The following year Colthurst entered into partnership with Welsh-born Myddelton (there are various spellings of his name used in a variety of historical accounts), who had made his name and fortune in cloth-making, banking and as goldsmith to James I.

New River Head

By 1613 some 38,000 gallons of fresh water, having made the 38-mile journey from Hertfordshire, were arriving every day at the New River Head, close to where today's Sadler's Wells Theatre stands. And it was Myddelton, not Colthurst or Inglebert, who would go down in history as the driving force behind this engineering marvel of its day, having a grand statue erected in his honour at Islington Green and a number of public houses named after him.

Among these was the Myddelton's Head, which opened in 1614 and was sited on 'the west end of a paved avenue on the south of Sadler's Wells Theatre', according to Walter Thornbury in his *Old London* of 1872. In 1831 it became the Sir Hugh Myddelton Tavern, closing finally in 1882.

By then the Myddleton Arms (please note spelling), was well established in Canonbury Road, having been trading here since the 1830s. The route of the New River runs close by. A former Courage house, the current building is mid-Victorian and has a nice frontage of frosted glass. It seems likely that George Orwell, a great fan of the humble public house, would have popped in for a quick one during his time living around the corner in Canonbury Square.

47. THE CORONET, Nos 338–346 Holloway Road, N7

Since they were founded in 1979 by Tim Martin, the JD Wetherspoons chain have made something of an art form of converting disused banks and cinemas into grand, large-scale pubs. The Coronet in Holloway Road was one of their earliest.

It first opened its doors as a pub on 14 March 1996, the latest chapter in a long, eventful and sometimes troubled history for this elegant (late) art deco structure.

Today's Coronet began life as the Savoy Cinema on 5 February 1940, part of the ABC (Associated British Cinemas) chain. Work had started on the building a few years beforehand and when the Second World War started in September 1939, it was decided to continue with the project as completion was within sight.

The Savoy was designed by William Riddell Glen, prolific staff architect for the ABC chain, and was a single-screen cinema with a capacity of 1,826.

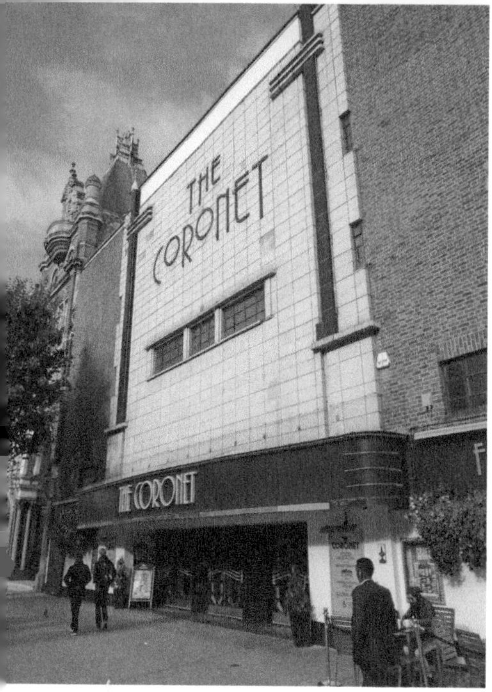

The Coronet, Holloway Road.

End of Cinema

In 1962 it was renamed the ABC and in 1979 was leased to the small independent Coronet chain of cinemas. However it appears that the writing was already on the wall for this particular movie theatre and following a double bill of *Blade Runner* and *Body Heat,* screened on 22 June 1983, it closed for business, bringing the safety curtain down on forty years of continuous use.

The following year the main auditorium was converted into a snooker hall with a false ceiling blocking it off from the splendour of the balcony above. This space gradually fell into disrepair, becoming a place of refuge for much of north London's pigeon population. The old foyer operated for a time as an amusement arcade.

In 1996, after much conversion work and careful restoration, The Coronet reopened as a pub with many of the original fixtures and fittings retained. It has remained one of Holloway Road's most popular watering holes ever since and gets extremely busy when Arsenal are playing at the nearby Emirates Stadium.

In August 2016, The Coronet was listed as an asset of community value (ACV) by Islington Council following an application by the local branch of the Campaign for Real Ale (CAMRA). Richard Lewis, who led the application, told the *Islington Tribune*: 'The Coronet is accessible and affordable and it caters for all ages, particularly the elderly.'

The Coronet made less positive newspaper headlines in November 2016, when Wetherspoons agreed to pay damages totalling £44,000 to a group of Irish travellers who were refused entry to the pub by security staff.

There is rarely a dull moment when it comes to the Holloway Road.

48. THE SCOTTISH STORES, Nos 2–4 Caledonian Road, N1

There seems to be no end in sight to the 'hipsterisation' of London, as a stroll along the Caledonian Road will confirm. This famous old north London thoroughfare, running

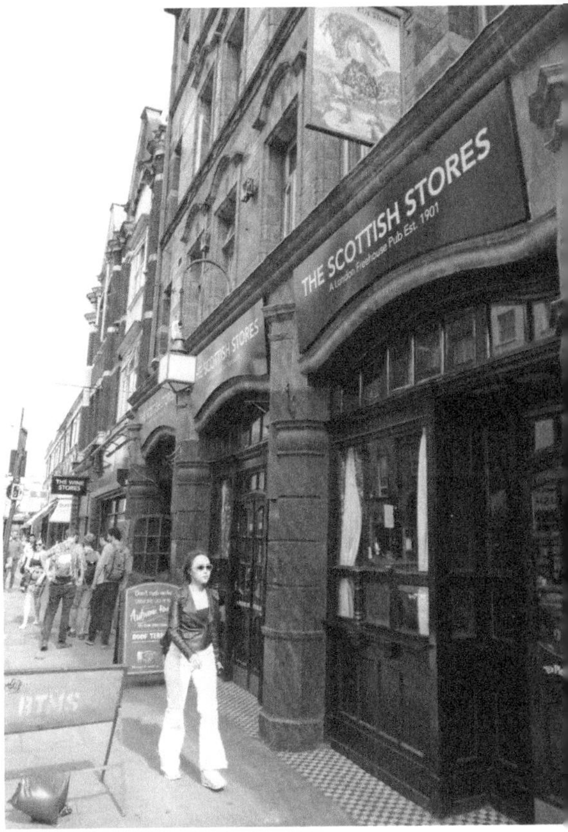

Right: The Scottish Stores, Caledonian Road.

Below: Arts and Craft-inspired interior of The Scottish Stores.

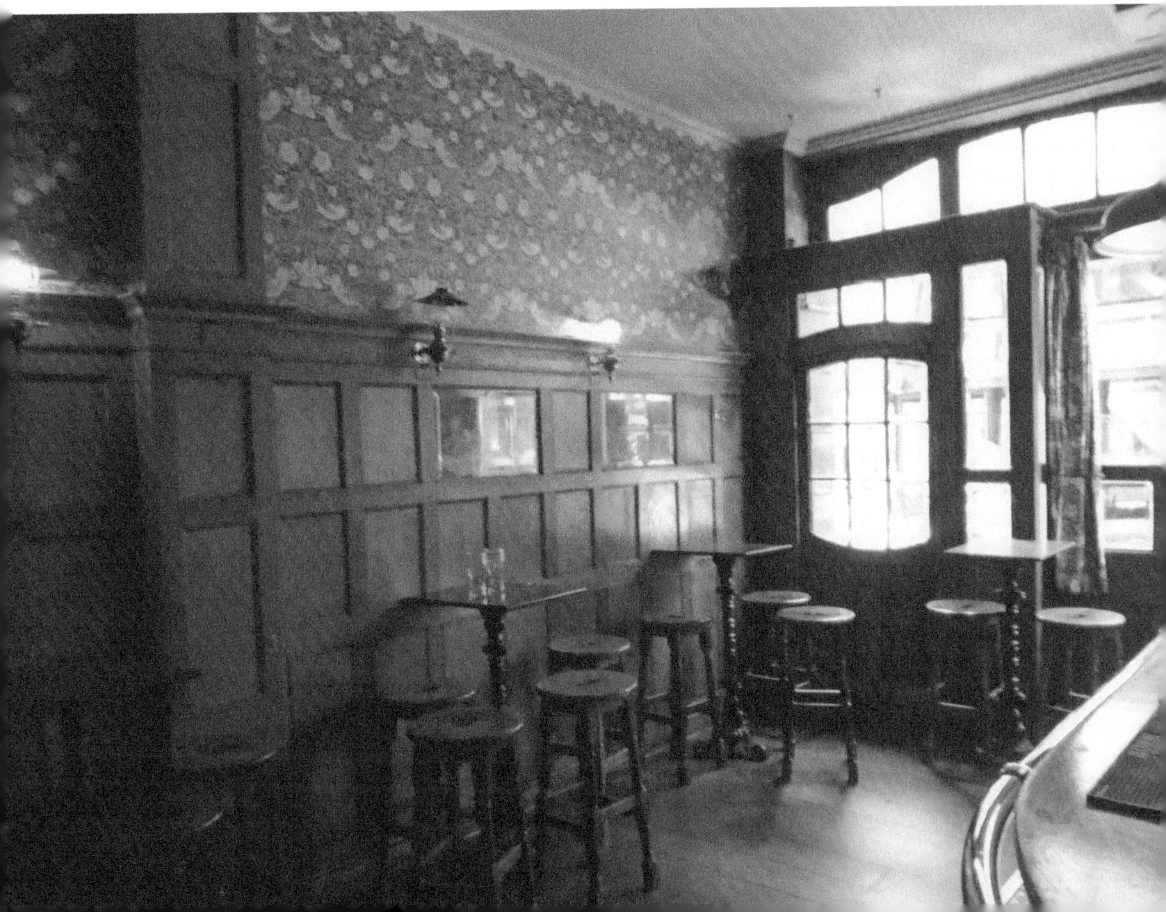

from Pentonville Road to Holloway Road, has long been known as a distinctly down-to-earth, working-class enclave, a perpetually gloomy but strangely life-assuring stretch of Islington. But, as a visit to The Scottish Stores, close to the junction with Pentonville Road, will confirm, the times they are a changing.

King's Cross and the surrounding streets were once a notorious red-light district, but hand in hand with the magnificent restoration of St Pancras and the remarkable reimagining of King's Cross station itself, the area has shed much of its former seedy image.

For generations of people who know this stretch of the capital, today's Scottish Stores will be remembered as the Flying Scotsman. As such it had a reputation as a rough and ready place, famous – or infamous, depending on your point of view – for staging striptease in a side room, which now houses a wine bar. My own abiding memories of the Flying Scotsman are of broken windows and sawdust on the barroom floor.

Orignal Name

The Flying Scotsman closed its doors for the last time in November 2015, reopening the following month as The Scottish Stores, a welcome return for the pub's original name. The emphasis now is on craft and cask beer.

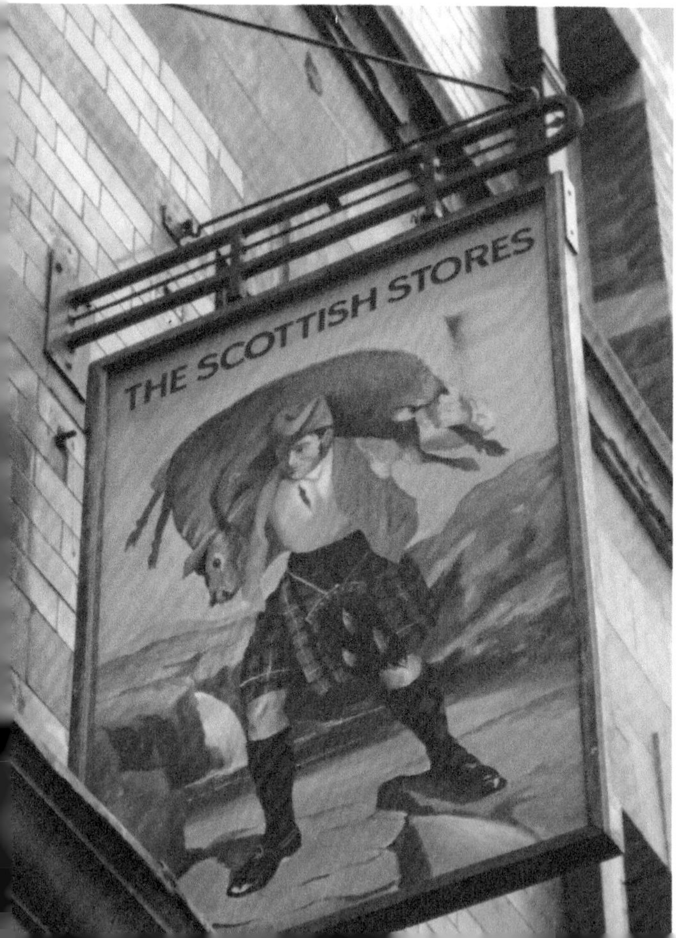

The Scottish Stores.

Quoted in the local *Islington Tribune* at the time, Caledonian ward councillor Paul Convery said, 'There will be people who will scream gentrification but this will be much better than what is there now.'

Grade II listed, the building was designed by prolific architects Wylson and Long for the theatre and pub speculator James Kirk. Wylson and Long are perhaps best known for the grand Oxford Music Hall, which stood on the corner of Oxford Street and Tottenham Court Road until its demolition in 1926. Kirk also had a hand in that venture.

The Scottish Stores, part of a development that stretches around the corner into Pentonville Road, is positively restrained by comparison, although its interior has a certain solid charm about it and has some nice Arts and Craft touches, not to mention some impressive original portioning screens complete with etched glass. There's also a fine cartouche with the inscription 'The Scottish Stores 1901'.

This was one of Kirk's very last ventures, for like many pub speculators of the time he overextended himself and was declared bankrupt in 1901. Fortunately The Scottish Stores opened anyway and, I am glad to report, is still very much with us today.

Acknowledgements

There are, as ever, a number of people I would like to thank for helping, in one way or another, with this book. I am, once again, grateful to Robert Elms, his producer Sarah Bateson and the rest of the team at BBC Radio London. They have put up with me for many years, and continue to do so. I am proud to be associated with a radio show that has become something of a London institution. I must also mention my good friends Stevie Cox and Alan Higham, who I see only occasionally these days but spent many years traipsing the highways and byways of Clerkenwell and Islington with, 'researching' the rich pub heritage of this most unique quarter of the mighty metropolis. Mention should also go to my sister Karen and nephew Connor, who continue to live in the area, and also my late parents, in particular my dad, who first introduced me to the joys of the great London pub. Most of all, however, I must mention my wife Lydia, who once again proofed my copy, and also my daughter Harriet, who in her unique way offered encouragement throughout. I am nothing without them. And I must not forget the fine citizens of the Peoples' Republic of Finsbury, past, present and future. *Altiora petimus*. Always.

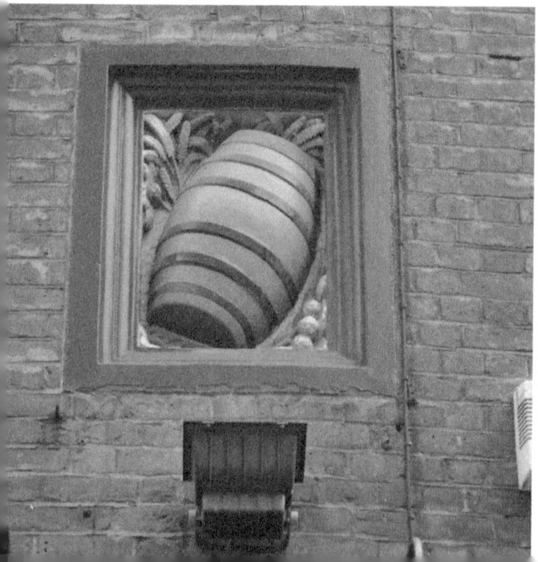

Exterior detail from the One Tun,
Saffron Hill.

GLORY DAYS
STEAM IN EAST ANGLIA

PETER SWINGER

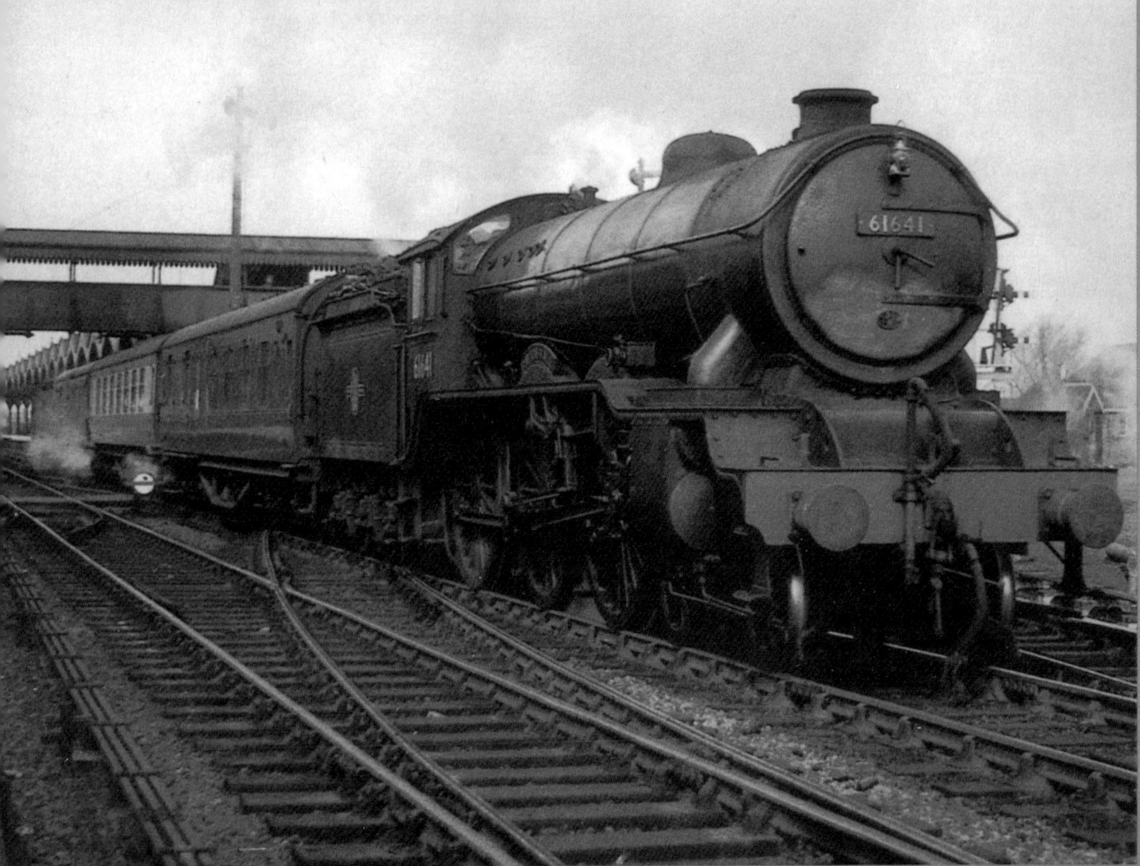